THE CHINA DREAM:
GUANGDONG STORY

中国梦·广东故事

INNOVATION

创新的广东

CHEN XIANG

TRANSLATED BY FENG HONGLIN

SPM
Southern Publishing & Media Co.Ltd.
Guangdong People's Publishing House Ltd.

Editors: Li Jie, Wang Ning
Published by Guangdong People's Publishing House Ltd., China
www.gdpph.com

First published 2017
Printed in the People's Republic of China

The China Dream: Guangdong Story- Innovation/ Chen Xiang and translated by Feng Honglin
ISBN 978-7-218-11891-8 (paperback, 1st edition)

Preface

Located in southern China, Guangdong Province is the first region in China to implement the reform and opening up, and it is also one of the most affluent areas nationwide. The Pearl River, China's third largest river, runs across the whole province. The Pearl River Delta is an alluvial plain flushed by the Pearl River. After nearly 40 years of rapid development, it has already become one of the most important city groups of China. The Hong Kong Special Administrative Region, and the Macao Special Administrative Region adjoin to Guangdong Province. With the natural geographical relations and the same cultural background, they constitute China's unique Guangdong–Hong Kong–Macao Greater Bay Area—a world–class vigorous economic and cultural area.

For nearly 40 years of rapid development, Guangdong has been playing a leading role in innovation, spurring the rapid development of new growth drivers. There are many rapidly grown–up enterprises in Guangdong, such as Huawei, Tencent, and UMi, which have become important engines of Guangdong's new economy development. Huawei and Tencent are now widely known in China. We try to approach such enterprises and their employees, to find the "secret" of the most innovative and cutting–edge development in Guangdong.

Guangdong has been the most dynamic foreign trade area in China since ancient times. And Guangzhou has been a commercial city through the ages, as well as an important interconnecting city alongside the "Maritime Silk Road". Foreigners from all over the world travel across major cities in Guangdong everyday, sightseeing, attending business meetings, studying or visiting friends. In Guangzhou, there are a large number of foreigners from Europe, America, Southeast Asia, the Middle East, Africa and other places, doing business here everyday. They ship back clothing, fabric, seafood, electrical appliances or glasses; foreign trade is booming. In the Shenzhen Special Economic Zone ports, people and vehicles travelling between Hong Kong and Shenzhen are always lined up. Foreigners living here for many years gradually adopt and merge into customs and culture of Guangdong, and regard Guangdong as their "second home". Meanwhile, tens of millions of workers from other provinces live in Guangdong, especially in the Pearl River Delta, where they work in factories, earn money to support their families, and try to realize their own dreams and ambitions. Whether foreigners or migrant workers, they are all practitioners, promoters and witnesses of Guangdong's reform and opening up. We conduct close observation of their work and life to record their ups and downs.

Ten years ago, the per capita income in the Pearl River Delta had already reached the level of that of moderately developed countries, and it is moving towards high–income phase. But the embarrassment is that in the eastern, western and northern parts of Guangdong Province, there are still large number of underdeveloped rural areas, and some places are even in extreme poverty, which distresses successive provincial governments. The government is determined to carry out large–scale "poverty alleviation" action, and vows to lift all peasants of impoverished areas out of poverty in three years, and promote common prosperity in these parts of Guangdong like the Pearl River Delta.

As the most populated, dynamic, and developed province that has been spearheading reform and opening up, recent practices in Guangdong are full of strength and sweetness. We go into it, and hope to find and record those breathtaking, touching and impressive stories of the development in Guangdong these years. Those people and those stories constitute a glaring part in the glittering development of the new era in Guangdong.

Through these stories, you can see diligence and endeavors of Guangdong people in the process of modernization. Through the perspective of Guangdong, you can see great efforts of Chinese people in realizing the China dream of the great rejuvenation of the Chinese nation.

总序

广东省位于中国南部，是中国最早实行改革开放的区域，也是目前中国最富庶的地区之一。中国的第三大河流珠江穿越广东省全境，由珠江冲积而成的珠江三角洲在经过近40年迅速发展后，已经成为中国最重要的城市群之一。香港特别行政区、澳门特别行政区与广东省毗邻，天然的地缘和一脉相承的人文情缘，构成了中国独有的粤港澳大湾区——一个世界级活跃的经济人文区域。

和中国其他地区一样，在经过长达近40年的高速发展之后，广东面临产业转型升级转变发展动能的重任，创新驱动成为推动此轮变革的重要抓手。广东省内有许多近年来快速成长起来的新型企业，比如华为、腾讯、有米科技，它们成为广东新经济发展的重要引擎。华为和腾讯，以及它们的“老板”任正非和马化腾，在中国几乎家喻户晓。我们试图走近这样的企业及其员工，找到广东创新驱动最前沿的发展“密码”。

广东自古以来是中国对外商贸最活跃的地区，广州是千年商都，是“海上丝绸之路”重要的节点城市。来自世界各地的外国人每天往来于广东省内各大城市，他们或旅游观光，或商务会议，或求学访友。在广州，每天大量来自欧美、东南亚、中东和非洲等地的外国人在这里做生意，他们把这里的服装、布匹、海产品、电器或者眼镜托运回国，外贸做得红红火火。在深圳经济特区口岸，进出香港和深圳的车辆、人流常常排成长龙。长年生活在这里的外国人，在生活习俗和文化上逐渐接受并慢慢融入广东，广东成为他们的“第二故乡”。与此同时，更多的数千万计的来自中国内地的普通劳工常年生活在广东尤其是珠江三角洲地区，他们在工厂里“打工”，凭借“打工”挣下的钱养家糊口，并试图实现自己的人生梦想。无论是外国人还是农民工，他们都是广东改革开放的实践者、推动者和见证者。我们近距离观察他们的工作和生活，记录他们的喜怒哀乐。

珠江三角洲地区早在10年前人均收入便已达到中等发达国家水平，正迈向高收入阶段。但令人尴尬的是，在广东省的东、西、北部仍有大片生活并不富裕的农村，一些地方甚至还处于贫困状态，这让广东省历届政府颇感头痛。政府下决心开展大规模的“扶贫”行动，并发誓要在3年后让所有贫困地区的农民摆脱贫困，力促粤东西北地区与珠江三角洲地区走向共同富裕。

作为人口最多、经济最活跃、总量最大、地处改革开放前沿的省份，广东近年的实践既具有力量又让人感到温馨。我们深入其中，希望通过我们去发现去记录，在广东发展这些年中，那些或动人心魄或充满温情或饱含人性的故事。那些人，那些事，终将构成广东新时期史诗般发展历程中炫目的一环。

通过这些故事，人们可以看见，在现代化进程中广东人的奋发图景；透过广东，可以看见中国人民为实现中华民族伟大复兴的中国梦的奋斗历程。

Contents

Contents

目　录

目 录

A Penguin Who Changes the World

Pony Ma's Three Crises

In September 1987, Zorn, a German professor, attended a technology symposium in Beijing. After a series of conditioning, he managed to connect the Institute of Computer Application Technology of Beijing with the Computer Center of Karlsruhe University by the computer.

On 14th September, Zorn and Wang Yunfeng, a Chinese professor, drafted an e-mail together, saying "Across the Great Wall we can reach every corner in the world," and "This is the

On the evening of 14th September 1987, in the Institute of Computer Application Technology of Beijing, a dozen people gathered around a big Siemens Computer, among whom we found Professor Wang Yunfeng and Professor Zorn.

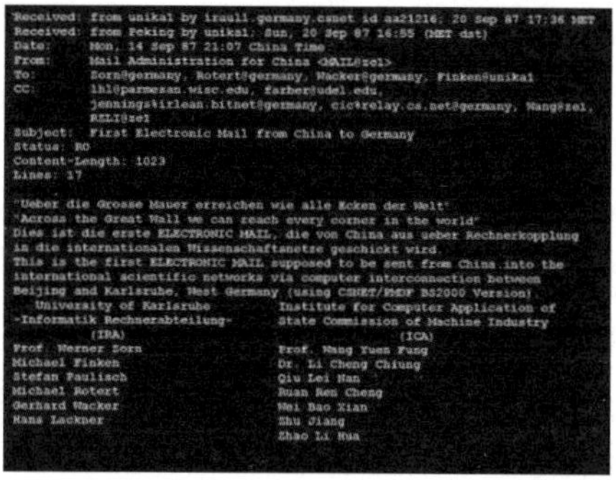

```
Received: from unikal by iraul1.germany.csnet id aa21216; 20 Sep 87 17:36 MET
Received: from Peking by unikal; Sun, 20 Sep 87 16:55 (MET dst)
Date:     Mon, 14 Sep 87 21:07 China Time
From:     Mail Administration for China <MAIL@zel>
To:       Zorn@germany, Rotert@germany, Wacker@germany, Finken@unikal
CC:       lhl@parmesan.wisc.edu, farber@udel.edu,
          jennings%irlean.bitnet@germany, cic%relay.cs.net@germany, Wang@zel,
          RZLI@zel
Subject:  First Electronic Mail from China to Germany
Status: RO
Content-Length: 1023
Lines: 17

"Ueber die Grosse Mauer erreichen wie alle Ecken der Welt"
"Across the Great Wall we can reach every corner in the world"
Dies ist die erste ELECTRONIC MAIL, die von China aus ueber Rechnerkopplung
in die internationalen Wissenschaftsnetze geschickt wird.
This is the first ELECTRONIC MAIL supposed to be sent from China into the
international scientific networks via computer interconnection between
Beijing and Karlsruhe, West Germany (using CSNET/PMDF BS2000 Version).
   University of Karlsruhe              Institute for Computer Application of
-Informatik Rechnerabteilung-           State Commission of Machine Industry
          (IRA)                                        (ICA)
Prof. Werner Zorn                       Prof. Wang Yuen Fung
Michael Finken                          Dr. Li Cheng Chiung
Stefan Paulisch                         Qiu Lei Nan
Michael Rotert                          Ruan Ren Cheng
Gerhard Wacker                          Wei Bao Xian
Hans Lackner                            Zhu Jiang
                                        Zhao Li Hua
```

The first e-mail sent from China.

First Electronic Mail from China to Germany", of which the title and content are both written in English and German. It is the famous e-mail later known as "Across the Great Wall, to the World".

In addition to the professors, Wang Yunfeng and Zorn, there were 11 participants from China and Germany who also signed on the e-mail.

But there was a problem in the e-mail server CSNET that one bug in the PMDF agreement led to a dead cycle, which delayed the successful sending of that e-mail. After consultations, they received confirmation from the CSNET Information Center that there was always the problem, especially when the phone circuit worked badly. Professor Zorn's assistant Michael Finken, staying in Beijing and Gerd Wacker, staying in Kurlsruh, worked together to make up with software for the unstable signal confusion, overcoming many obstacles such as working jet leg. Seven days later, on 20th September, that e-mail finally reached Germany, crossing half of the globe.

By now, the 45-year old Pony Ma, who comes from Shantou, Guangdong Province, has created TENCENT for over 18 years. Dating back to a few months ago, 11th November 2016 was the 18th anniversary of TENCENT. On that day, Pony Ma, together with the CEO office staff, sent out WeChat red packets to current employees, former employees, outsourcing employees and company service personnel, totaling at 30 million yuan.

But that was not the climax. Pony Ma later announced a decision that they would give each current employee 300 TENCENT stocks. Calculated by TENCENT's stock price of 200 HK dollars per stock, the bonus they planned to give out this time was worth 1.5 billion yuan.

Of course, TENCENT's stock price is a mythic legend. On 16th June 2004, TENCENT Holding was officially listed, opening on that very day at 4.375 HK dollars, which has accumulatively increased by 250 times twelve years later.

"QQ's Father" Pony Ma has an appearance of Confucian elegance and is of gentle and modest character.

Because of the development of mobile phones, China has become the country where the internet including mobile internet is most widespread in the world. In Pony Ma's concept, during the last five years, TENCENT has evolved through a closed environment into an open environment and has become a real interconnected eco-system. "Some former internal business lines which did not perform well have been cut, sold or given away, only the most nuclear telecommunication and digital content is retained, including the 'internet+' which is being promoted now. The so-called '+' is to fully cooperate with other enterprises."

Judged from its market value of more than 230 billion dollars, TENCENT is now the biggest internet company in Asia. This entrepreneur, who calls himself as a typical "programming ape (programmer)" and who never thought of setting up a company, behaves very modestly on many occasions, even when he is with close friends or the family. "In these 18 years of TENCENT, what I more frequently say is thank you. Thank you, all my colleagues."

In fact, he is holding in hand a stupendous user group and a giant business empire. The number of monthly active users of TENCENT's WeChat and QQ has respectively reached 806 million and 899 million, while in 2016, the total population of mainland China was only 1.38271 billion.

His appearance is of Confucian elegance and he looks very gentle. But this "QQ's Father" always has a very strong marketing ability accompanied by very deep crisis awareness. When commenting on his experiences of business development, the media always use such words as awestruck, creative and open, etc.

According to Pony Ma, TENCENT met three biggest difficulties in its development history.

The first difficulty occurred at the financing period of its initial stage. At the beginning of development, TENCENT team went through the toughest time of biding failure and lacking money to buy servers to meet the overgrowing number of users. But this kind of difficulties also forced TENCENT team to think about how to generate blood to support its growth from very early on.

The second difficulty was the competition with MSN. "Other people all thought at you were to die, the only question was when. But we survived. Our products were made to meet Chinese users' habits better than foreign products." It was because TENCENT made a lot of modifications by taking China's internet condition and Chinese users' habits into consideration that it won the war against MSN.

The third obstacle occurred five years ago before WeChat was born, when TENCENT was faced with a very big pressure since Sina Weibo turned from social media to social network.

Of course, the biggest crisis in TENCENT's history should be the "3Q War" in 2010. The disputes between QIHU 360 and TENCENT had been a long story originating from the "jostles" of their "star products" in 2012. On 27th September 2010, QIHU 360 issued its newly developed "privacy protector" which focused on collecting information about QQ's invasions of users' privacy. Soon afterwards, QQ immediately pointed out that 360 explorer was suspected to make promotion through pornographic websites. On 3rd November 2012, TENCENT announced that all the computers with 360 software installed should stop running QQ software, and users were allowed to log in QQ only when they had unloaded 360 software, forcing users to make an "either-or" selection.

On their own interests, these two companies started a series internet wars from 2010 to 2014 and ended up with lawsuits.

They sued each other for three times with QIHU 360 lost in the end, among which QIHU 360's monopoly charge against TENCENT caught most attention. On the morning of 16th October 2014, the Supreme People's Court decided that TENCENT's QQ did not occupy a dominant position in market and rejected QIHU's appeal, maintaining the judgment of the first trial.

On 5th December of the same year, Pony Ma announced that TENCENT would enter into a preparation period of strategic reformation which would last for half a year. He said: "'monopoly' is an irritating charge. In most cases, it is an imagined enemy, something that does not

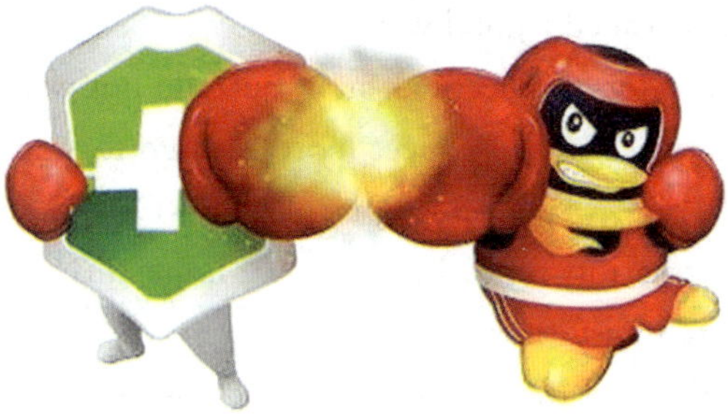

Memory of the war between TENCENT and 360 remains fresh in netizens' mind.

exist. In the 90s of the 20th century, we could see that in our IT industry Microsoft was the company which was most criticized and charged against in the name of monopoly. When the era of internet came, what problems was Microsoft faced with? We saw a lot of new companies still able to stand out. It was hardly possible that all creators and all entrepreneurs thought that they had no future. What chance was left when Microsoft might enter many areas and occupy the first position in many industries? But we all witnessed what actually happened in the following years. We saw the rising of not only Google but also eBay. In particular, Google was a very powerful company which could do everything, getting involved in all internet product lines. Still we saw the rising of Facebook. When Facebook started to think that there was no other threats to challenge its position in the market of social network and interpersonal relationship, we saw the rising of a new form—Weibo.

Pony Ma said with a little grievance, "So, we can see that a lot of the so-call monopoly companies are still faced with huge crises when the industry is continuously experiencing reforms. That is to say, in the industry of which the value changes rapidly, there is not a single company can rest easy. So, to challenge Alibaba, Baidu and TENCENT which are called three big mountains, the best way is not to build up a similar platform to create monopoly but to follow the trend to form a good industrial chain. Only that can be called a good way. "

"Looking back, I could gain a lot of reflections on it, but I do not want to indulge myself in all the disputes, what I expect more is to go forward and look forward." Pony Ma said, that dispute pushed TENCENT to make reformation and transformation more firmly. "We hope this is a prudent, thorough and complete transformation."

Soon thereafter, TENCENT sold the business lines such as searching and e-commerce one after another in the form of investment, and focused on the basic connecting service of internet public affairs.

A Magic Path from Imitation, to Public Enemy, and to Industry Leader

When commenting on TENCENT's development path, IT commenters concluded: "TENCENT has been created for 18 years, walking through a magic path from imitation, to public enemy and to industry leader."

In 1984, Pony Ma was brought by his parents to Shenzhen. He received secondary and high education in Shenzhen Middle school and Shenzhen University. After graduation, he worked for a telecommunication company in Shenzhen for 6 years, and then started a business with his middle school and university classmates and one peer from telecommunication industry, 5 persons in total.

Penguin is TENCENT's brand image.

At that time, the total number of netizens in China was only 3 million.

In the year of 1999, nearly nobody could be definitely sure about how big an imagination could the internet development bring to people. At the very beginning, internet was most often applied as technology and was accessed by only a few people. Such a thing that only existed at technical level could hardly inspire people's imagination. Under such background, in the dilemma of buying a house or starting a business, it was obviously Pony Ma's foresight of internet and IM that made Pony Ma resolutely and determinately discover internet and develop QQ. Even Lei Jun also refused to invest in TENCENT at that time.

You can say that Pony Ma made QQ by accident since it was a side product of telecom products. But that opinion could not explain why soon thereafter QQ could surpass OICQ which was IM's ace product in a very short time in terms of server storage and personal images, etc. Those products may seem very ordinary to us now, but they were great creations at that time, just as WeChat that we are using now.

Earlier or later, QQ might not have succeeded. But it grasped the first bonus of the initial stage of China internet, which laid a solid foundation for TENCENT's being listed later on and even for the present social empire.

At the preliminary stage of the start–up period, TENCENT made right actions at several critical moments.

TENCNET Logo, penguin image at the center.

The first was the operator's bonus. Though QQ gained a lot of users at the initial stage, how to earn money was obviously a big problem at that time. After all, the capital market still held a very conservative attitude toward internet and there was no such a saying as market dream rate. The financing passing industry chain was not mature at that time and enterprises had not enough financial support to say that, "We do not think of profit for the moment." At that moment, QQ grasped the life–saving straw, the operator, and took advantages of that opportunity to turn around.

At that time, SP business, which could be said as the earliest way for internet enterprises to make money, saved QQ's life to a large extent. Without those SP businesses, QQ might have been sold at 1 million yuan. With that income, QQ could not only support its own operation, but also laid a good foundation for its being listed later on. At that time internet enterprises still could not easily get capital investment under the condition that they had not made profit yet. While doing SP, QQ itself performed relatively well. On one hand, QQ developed functions of value–added capacity such as membership and QQ show, on the other hand, QQ started to issue Q currency which is up to now the only hard currency that can rival telephone card. SP business declined in the end, but QQ grasped the critical opportunity and got rid of the predicament at this round.

The second was the explosion period of PC applications. In 2005, after TENCENT was listed, QQ had nearly become a gigantic product. It was an explosion period of desk software such as TTPlayer, Baofeng Video Player, Xunlei, input method, etc. which were listed as must–installed softwares for a computer. Under such condition, TENCENT, by using the powerful resource distributing channels of QQ, started to develop a series of similar products such as QQ Video Player, QQ Music, QQ Explorer and QQ Input Method, etc. Though QQ was criticized by the whole industry, we can see it clearly that many of TENCENT's current

TENCENT products.

horizontally developed products are based on what were made at that round, such as the newly independent QQ Music and the QQ Explorer which has ranked among the top explorers in market share. In addition, it was also during this period that QQ beat MSN. It might not be known to many that MSN used to have a bigger market share than QQ at its golden age.

TENCENT also took advantages of the opportunity to launch web portal, which was under the shadow of three big web portals at that time. But TENCENT web portal fought hardly by using QQ resources such as mini pop–ups and tips etc., and finally managed to become the fourth biggest web portal after Sina, Sohu and NetEase. That's strategically meaningful to TENCENT. In addition to certain speech right, the web portal also laid a foundation for the upcoming QQ Live and QQ Sports.

Web portal advertising was internet enterprises' second important income resource following value–added service. The foundations that QQ had laid at this period not only provided a space for future development, but also constructed a strategic defense.

The third was the game window. Chen Tianqian's Shanda pushed the internet into an era of "digging gold with excavator". Internet entrepreneurs finally discovered another fastest and most profitable way of making money in addition to value–added service and advertising. TENCENT luckily grasped what has become the most important revenue resource up to now. But at the beginning, it was not so easy for TENCENT to enter into the domain of games. The first few games did not stand out selling well, and were even unknown to most people. It was not until TENCENT discovered games of playing cards that the platform developed by TENCENT quickly defeated Ourgame and became the hottest platform, in which QQ's social relationship chain found its true value. And it was also from that time that TENCENT started to realize the natural compatibility of social contact and games. In view of the success of card games, TENCENT continued to launch some other successful games such as DNF, then CF, to current LOL. Now TENCENT has acquired half of market share in the domain of games.

The most important was that TENCENT grasped the chance at the explosion period of social network. The sudden rising of Facebook inspired many internet companies, and a number of websites grew up very rapidly, including the former Xiaonei Web and Happy Web. At that time, the social characters of those websites could even be compared to QQ as horse and horse. But QQ had a most important Ace—QQ Space. I remember reading a statistics that even at its best time the market share and user share of Renren Web (the former Xiaonei Web) of social platform was not at the same level as that of QQ. Games such as stealing vegetables and moving cars were very hot at that time, but the rapid response of QQ Space won the users immediately. Until now, many people will still ask a question: “Why there is no Facebook in China?” In my opinion, QQ’s blocking actions against Renren Web and Happy Web by using QQ Space completely destroyed the dream of having Facebook in China. The rapid development of QQ Space did not only help QQ transform from IM to an integrated social platform, but also laid a foundation for the upcoming Feeds advertising. The Feeds advertisements in QQ Space are considered as the best quality resources by many enterprises.

What is the Next Creation that Will Influence the World?

At the initial stage of starting a business, leadership was totally out of Pony Ma's consideration, and what was most important to him was to keep the company surviving. He said: "Both of my parents never expected a nerd like me could be able to start up a

The penguin puts on hundreds of thousands of images, playing different roles.

business. So the first step was to find partners. They could make up for my shortcomings."

Among the partners he had found, Xu Chenye, Zhang Zhidong, and Chen Yidan were his middle school or university classmates, and Zeng Liqing was his former colleague. They all had different strong points which were well complementary to each other. What Pony Ma needed to do was to "make full use of each one's strong points and balance each one's opinions." He was not a bossing CEO and he did not decide all things of management. At the early stage, the partners often sit together for two or three hours with one pot of chicken rice on each one's hand, discussing business affaires at the table. Many company's important decisions were made on such occasions. Eating chicken rice was a symbol of TECENT's partnership culture. Even when the partners gradually stepped out from the first line management, they still maintained very good interactions without making any disharmonious voices or events. Chen Yidan's explanation was that the partners were from similar family backgrounds, which resulted in the fact that they were of similar characters. They were all relatively gentle and prudent and can accept negotiation mechanism instead of pursuing

The old building of TENCENT headquarter.

personal heroism.

But since the internet keeps changing every second, how can TENCENT Empire keep being creative? That is what Pony Ma must face.

In 2010, all the people were contending for ship tickets to get aboard the mobile internet. That was a war of either to die or to survive. The companies such as Baidu and 360 were deemed to be faced with a risk of being left behind since they failed to bring out products that had real influential power. TENCENT's condition was also not very good, with Weibo aiming at the social network and QQ bearing a heavy history burden when transforming from PC to mobile. Pony Ma confessed that it was the biggest crisis they had ever encountered.

At that time, three TENCENT internal teams engaged in the development of revolutionary products. The one who solved the mobile phone terminal problem would be the winner. Finally, QQ Postbox team developed a client end product which could quickly receive and send e—mails through mobile phones. So quickly that the user would think it was not an e—mail. That product was what we called WeChat later. Allen Zhang, its developer, became the father of WeChat.

In TENCENT, they were used to the fact that competitors might be their colleagues. Pony Ma did not consider it as a problem; instead he even thought that good internal competition was very necessary. "You will work hard only when you are beaten by yourself. And it ensures that the company will not lose some big strategic chances."

In 2013, interviewed by CCTV at a dialogue show, Pony Ma claimed that they had got a standing ticket for the mobile internet. In June 2016, he said, the ship had already pulled in before we could sit down, and it was to set foot on a new land. A new round of technological innovation represented by the artificial intelligence was the future trend, on which internet giants including TENCENT were working hard at a faster pace.

Witnessing the contest between AlphaGo and human, Pony Ma and his team all felt very excited. They were eager to do something at this new age of technology after so many years of dreariness.

Storing 3.5 million applications and distributing 2 million per day, AppQQ version 7.0 will add a robot function based on AI and iCloud, so that users can call a taxi without loading Didi Taxi in the future. TENCENT will make more research and development based on AI, and will make it open to more partners.

Even so, Pony Ma still does not know what will be the next creation that will influence the world. "Every big reformation is accompanied with the change of device. The whole eco–system becomes different in consequence of the popularity of smartphones. New changes will occur

The new building of TENCENT headquarter.

in application situations as VR and AR devices become more and more popular in the future.

Ever since he went to school, Pony Ma always loved astronomy which had not direct connection with his business but did affect how he thought to some extent. He said: "The Love for astronomy would make you feel so small that we may always be an accident in the universe. That would make you become more optimistic and think that it is not a big deal whatever you are facing."

Artist Allen Zhang and WeChat

Today, Chinese people's dependence on WeChat is almost extreme, which is also the excellent achievement of TENCENT Empire in the second decade of the new century.

Pony Ma recalled that at that time there were three teams making the WeChat product. It was reasonable to let another former business group of QQ to develop IM for mobile phones at this new chance. In addition, they were also developing mobile QQ, of which the original product structures were unreasonable, and then we quickly made adjustments to integrate all products, such as news and games, which were separated in PC and in mobile phone.

"Another one was the QQ Postbox Team at Guangzhou who has been engaged in mobile office since very early. So we started to consider whether we could develop an App in QQ Postbox to let every employee use mobile phone mail very conveniently. That team was required to develop a mobile mailbox. It was this team of 5 or 6 people that changed the mobile mail system into

WeChat. So WeChat was actually a mail system for quick short mails, of which the server in the back was the former postbox team. It only took one month or so for the team to produce a prototype. This team led by Allen Zhang has very strong product ability."

The WeChat icon.

"It did not arouse much attention when WeChat was newly launched. The real reasons for its popularity were as below. The first one was its voice function which similar foreign products lacked of, and it made the App become very popular in a short time. The second one was the matching with phone contacts. The first step was to link it with QQ contacts so as to make it survive. But the input of phone contacts would introduce many high-end users and increase the connection."

As a key person, Allen Zhang looks dark skinned and is a middle age man who likes playing golf. He is also commented by many people as "playing the role of an artist" most of the time and "he takes products as the artworks he creates." During these 17 years, Allen Zhang kept making self-replacement and self-upgrading. The Foxmail sold at 12 million yuan many years ago was a commercial failure rather than a product success. It was much more a pity that he lost a huge commercial opportunity in contrast with that money. That was Allen Zhang 1.0 associated with key words as product and technology. At the early stage of WeChat, he upgraded the tool to a platform, turned the simple requirement of serving users to guide their sentiments, and finished the second upgrade.

In the fall of 1998, Zhou Hongyi was introduced to Allen Zhang in Guangzhou for the first time. He saw this programmer who was already of some renown sitting with a dozen people in a small and old office surrounded by thick smoke. Seeing Zhou Hongyi, Allen Zhang put out the cigarette held in his hand and walked toward him with a poker face. The Foxmail developed by Zhang, which already had 2 million users, was the shareware that had the biggest group of users in China, while Zhou Hongyi was only a vice supervisor of the Research and Development Center of Founder Soft at that time.

Zhou Hongyi said, Foxmail had no commercial mode at that time, for which he always criticized Allen Zhang, and he suggested making profit by adding advertisements. Allen Zhang replied him by asking why he should do that. Feelings were all that he required. Each time, such kind of arguments was ended by Allen Zhang's longstanding silence. "How could such a person have developed WeChat?" Zhou Hongyi was confused.

When Foxmail was at its golden age, TENCENT only had a hundred thousand users, and many people considered mailbox as a bigger domain than social contact. When Pony Ma and Charles Zhang were excitedly looking for venture capital and making commercializations, Allen Zhang was often reading users' letters alone late at night. His hands would not leave the keyboard, always clicking the down arrow, watching letters flowing in front of his eyes one by one with none of them staying more than one second. In Allen Zhang's eyes, Foxmail had become a huge burden. Countless people were urging him to run forward every day, while the huge fame and user number did not bring him with any economic and social benefits.

One year later, Allen Zhang decided to sell Foxmail to a not very well-known internet company Boda. The night after the news was released, he wrote a letter full of sad sentiments, in which he described Foxmail to be an artwork he elaborately made. "From soul to appearance, I can count every detail and every story of it. In my heart, it has a soul because every section of its codes has my awareness when I was creating it. I suddenly feel an impulsion to recall my decision."

The login image of WeChat—a lonely person facing the blue planet Earth.

Artist Allen Zhang was always a lonely creator. In the past, he was walking freely on the broad runway until there occurred two obstacles—commerce and profit. While countless sharewares such as Maxthon, TTPlayer and Supper Rabbit were hit off the way, Allen Zhang luckily entered another runway. He was then only 31 years old, and many people thought that his personal legend seemed to end at that point.

That summer, Baidu was listed in NASDAQ. All thought there must be something wrong with their eyes, shocked by the fact that Baidu's stock was rising sharply from the issue price 27 dollars to 122.54 dollars with a boom of 354%. People had realized the power of capital and commerce, while Allen bought a car with the acquisition money that Boda gave him and went to Tibet where he was always longing for.

"How should I put it, this guy, is too naïve." said Zhou Hongyi. Such the entrepreneur who was famous for his being crafty and fighting in the commercial world commented on Allen Zhang who was even one year older.

Missing the first climax when internet was hitting NASDAQ, Boda started to decline. In 2005, Allen Zhang and Foxmail were sold to TENCENT as a package. Taking charge of QQ Postbox, Allen Zhang made it become the biggest mail service provider surpassing Net Ease mailbox. He just proved his product ability one more time.

In many times, the powerful ones were always businessmen, while most artists had to rely on businessmen's financial support and could not control their own lives. Foxmail brought Allen Zhang great fame and a very unstable destinies. He was always surrounded by businessmen. He made friends with them, and even wanted to learn from Microsoft how to make commercial operation, but he never set foot on commerce. At last, most of his friends who had both product–making and commercial talents all succeeded, such as Lei Jun, Zhou Hongyi, Pony Ma, and even the journalist Li Xueling who had interviewed him.

Someone commented that Allen Zhang was always following the trend, but he was not in it. From a programmer to a product manager, he learned to control his products, but he could never control users. But the generous destiny gave him a third chance, and this success was so great and was coming so fast.

Zen Ming was one of the 13 original team members. He said that nobody, including Allen Zhang, knew what WeChat should be made into at that time, not to mention that half of those members were interns who had zero experience. Their original target was to make it fast and stable, which was the same as what Allen Zhang had in mind when he was making Foxmail, a pure thinking of making tools. If Allen Zhang's product concept was stuck at that level, what he would make would be merely an acceptable chat tool.

Some colleagues compared Allen Zhang to a director who wanted to film a perfect block buster. It was not that he could not accept advertising implantation, but that he could not stand obvious implantation which would destroy the perfection. Wu Yi, who used to be the Assistant General Manager of Tenpay, described that when he met him for the first time three years ago, Allen Zhang was thinking about how to couple WeChat and commerce through payment: "He does not reject perfect cooperation, such as QQ Music, QQ Postbox and payment."

At the early stage of WeChat, Allen Zhang was responsible for product, while the commercial rules such as how to lead in the third party merchants and how to expand online and offline buisiness were all the responsibilities of Dai Zhikang, the vice president of TENCENT E-Commerce, and even the payment part was made to be done by the Tenpay team. At the end of 2012, Luo Yihang, the starter of Pingwest, wrote an article saying that the reason why WeChat was commercialized too slowly was due to the internal disputes between Zhang and Dai.

A series of events, such as Dai Zhikang's dismission, WeChat Payment's integration into WeChat after being separated from Tenpay, and the independence of WeChat business group, happened hereafter. You could consider them as the choice that Allen Zhang had made—since it was inevitable to commercialize WeChat, then WeChat team should take the lead in making the commercialization. At the same time, it also

Allen Zhang created WeChat after suffering from longstanding loneliness, perfectly combining the artist's feelings and the commercial profit making mode.

indicated that the TENCENT management represented by Pony Ma and Liu Zhi had made their choice that they chose to delegate Allen Zhang with a full charge of the commercialization.

Within the company, he took the control power over commercialization, and to the public, he tried to build up a new system to handle the relationship between art and commerce. For example, in TENCENT there used to be 120 projects queuing to be adopted into WeChat, while what WeChat required was to run them for one and a half months and then to make selection according to the statistics.

"WeChat includes the commercial actions such as launching what kind of functions and taking in what kind of cooperative partners as part of the product, while to many people, product is part of commerce." One of TENCENT's senior management told the journalist that you could interpret it as a commercialized value and an artist's methodology.

Even until today, TENCENT's commercial strategies are considered as relatively conservative. One insider gave his comments to the journalist that facing commercialization, Allen Zhang was experiencing an adapting process from escaping and attempting, to leading. He was never absolute.

WeChat payment increased common users' trading speed.

Allen Zhang's team.

He never promised anything that he was not able to do. He might even avoid talking about something that he was able to do.

The commercialization of WeChat shoulders the big dream of the whole TENCENT's transformation. For the moment, it is divided into three steps: the value-added service, e-commerce and O2O. Now only the first step is completed, while official accounts can realize the latter two steps simultaneously. Zen Ming says that WeChat will open more entrances and will provide the flow inlet expected by all merchants in the future.

Commenters used to conceive WeChat as merely a flow leading tool. But now by means of official accounts, WeChat connects TENCENT's powerful online marketing ability with offline business and has built up an enormous online + offline eco-system, in which all kinds of small eco-systems such as e-commerce, O2O, and healthcare service will emerge. The difference between WeChat and QQ can be compared to that between the real economy and the virtual economy, the latter is only less than 7% of the former.

In the past, Allen Zhang was used to stand behind businessmen, now he has come to the first line, following Pony Ma's path—being a product maker and a commercial leader at the same time. But commercial interests are huge and complicated. So we can imagine that Allen Zhang will still choose to keep silent in a long period of time.

Pony Ma recalled that when WeChat was newly launched, the operators became very nervous at the fact that nobody texted and people seldom made calls. "I would constrain you, and many countries around the world would make many rules to constrain you. But that was irresistible. I was always telling them that you should not be worried and you would definitely be benefited. Your voice service declined but your internet flow increased. How would that damage your profit? The growth was hard to predict. Till last year, statistics was growing faster than that of former voice service. They are now assured that the relationship between us is like that between fish and water. "

"Trumpchi",
Legend!

The Ambition of Entering America and a Car Named GS8

The first Trumpchi car rolled off the production line in Guangzhou seven years ago. At that time, in the second decade of the new century, the private car market was getting bigger and bigger in China.

Now, this auto brand, ranking the sixth in terms of sales volume in China, will be the first Chinese brand that is allowed to be exhibited in the main exhibition hall on the North American International Auto Show at the end of 2017. Observers believe that its major challenge of entering the American market is the high cost related to tests and to meeting the requirements of the highest safety & emission standard in the world. "The rules in the U.S. are too much stricter than that in China."

Guangzhou Automobile Group (hereinafter referred to as GAC) is performing better and better. In 2016, it was listed in Fortune Global 500 for the fourth consecutive year, ranking the 303rd, up by 59 compared to last year.

All around the world, its self-creative ability has become a salient representation of its regional competiveness. Today, the number of high-tech enterprises in Guangdong Province has ranked at the first position in China, achieving some targets of transforming old energy consumption to the new. The success of Trumpchi, the self-own automobile brand of Guangzhou automobiles, is the most shining page on the performance report on the automobile industry of Guangdong Province.

Up to now the total investment has accumulated to 13 billion yuan since 2005 when GAC planned to creat a self-own brand. GAC has built up a domestic first-class research and development center and a world-class plant producing vehicles and engines, and has launched its self-own brand Trumpchi. In the 2015 Report on Chinese New Vehicle Quality issued by J.D.Power, Trumpchi was the quality champion of Chinese brands for the third consecutive year, ranking the 8th along with GAC TOYOTA. As for its sales volume, Trumpchi has witnessed a jumping growth since it was launched into market in 2011 when the figure was 17 thousand, and 116 thousand in 2014. The sales volume of Tumpchi in 2015 was 190 thousand increasing by 63% year on year, while that of China vehicle market was only 4.7%. The total annual sales revenue

The automation level of production line for Trumpchi reaches at 60%.

was 17.7 billion yuan, and the monthly sales volume of GS4, the first Trumpchi SUV, managed to rank the top 3 among all SUVs of the whole China. It is said that a "1513" strategy has been included in the 13th Five-Year strategic planning initiated and implemented by GAC. The "1" key point is to develop self-own brands with the whole group's efforts and to realized jumping development of self-own brand business.

In 2016, Trumpchi made a "double breakthrough" of both sales volume and brand. On January 2017, Trumpchi kept on growing by riding on the momentum of last year's good performance. In January, the total sales volume of Trumpchi was 46273, increasing by 60% year on year, which ranked top among the domestic auto makers, pushing Chinese local brands to a higher level. Among the Trumpchis, the sales volume of GS8, the "flagship luxury huge 7-seat SUV" newly launched for only three months, was 9418 in January, greatly increasing for three consecutive months.

The single-month sales volume of GS8 was 9418, standing out along with Highlander and Edge in the sales market of median and large SUV. It was the first time that a Chinese local brand held a strong stance when fighting with its joint venture rivals face to face. It was also the first time in Chinese auto history that GS8 succeeded in the price range of 160000 to 250000 yuan where Chinese local brands had never reached before.

If keeping such high developing speed, GS8 is hopefully to surpass Highlander and Edge, and to become the top 1 in its market segment. The GS8 sales at the moment are also running toward this "small target". Once realized, it would undoubtedly be recorded in Chinese auto history, inspiring all the people who have been working hard for the rising of Chinese automobiles for more than 30 years and confirming their confidence in it.

Not only that, the hot sales of GS8 enabled Trumpchi to get rid of the embarrassment of walking by one leg. The hot-sale auto types increased from one to two, making the product structure approaching a reasonable status, and the price deviations of different types were further enlarged. It also pushed the sales weight of Trumpchin in GAC to increase from last year's 22.38% to 27.55%, increasing by 5% and approaching 30%.

Marked by GS8 hot sales, Trumpchi is leading Guangdong auto industry to transform from being "Made in Guangdong" to "Created in Guangdong" and to upgrade the reputation of "Made in Chia" from product to brand. In the near future, following the gradual development of its overseas strategies, especially its official landing in the US market in 2019, Trumpchi will also help to expand the reputation of "Chinese Brand" from the Chinese market to the global market. "Trumpchi will become the leading brand of Chinese autos. The annual sales plan of 1 million vehicles will be realized before the originally expected year 2020." On the eve of the 2017 North American International Auto Show, Yu Jun, Vice President of GAC Execution Committee and the General Manager of GAC Motor, made that prediction with great confidence.

CS4

The emergence of GS8 is definitely not accidental and not of any luck. It is the result of Trumpchi's insistence on high–end development strategies, on positive exploitation, and on international standard. From the original GA5, to GS5 & GS4, the price of Trumpchi is always the highest compared to that of all other local autos. The average unit price is even higher than that of some joint venture brands. Before the arrival of GS8, the average unit price of GS4 was around 140 thousand yuan. With the advent of GS8, the unit price of Trumpchi autos is directly increased to a brand new level of 200 thousand yuan, wining a broad strategic space for the upcoming auto types.

After being launched, the appearance design of GS8, which is "super hard and powerful", receives positive responses from both the media and consumers. However, the excellent appearance design is only one of the reasons why GS8 has gained such an excellent success. Trumpchi also provides "assured driving control at any terrains", "large seven–seat space", "new horizon and intelligent interconnection" and advanced quality with competitive price, which precede customers' expectation.

Since its being launched, GS8 has obtained nearly a hundred domestic and international awards such as "Annual China Brand SUV", "Annual Best Performing Large SUV", "Top 10 Highly Recommended New Autos 2016", and "Annual Most Popular SUV", and has been widely admired by the media and auto authorities, gaining good harvests of both sales and reputation.

At the same time, according to J.D. Power SM (IQS), Trumpchi brand has been the top 1 of China brands for four consecutive years. The quality of Trumpchi automobiles surpasses that of most joint venture products, and consumers' common trust becomes the internal factor for the hot sales of Trumpchi products.

In the market trend of consumption upgrading, brand attraction and

The new model of GS8 is of striking appearance.

product quality are playing more and more critical roles in the competition among auto enterprises. GS8 is fully loaded with the creative achievements made by Trumpchi in the domains of R&D, design and manufacturing.

In the Chinese market, an auto company obtains a market passport for the whole price range, once it can break into the market of prices range from CNY 200 to 250 thousand. TOYOTA and HONDA obtain a good share in the global mainstream vehicle market because of the hot sales of Camry and Accord. The success of GS8 is of milestone significance to Trumpchi, which makes it possible for Trumpchi to compete with Acura, Infinite and Cadillac, and enables it to fulfill its potentials in the market segments of Class B, A+, A and A0.

Trumpchi is not the first Chinese brand who insists on high-end product, and of course will not be the last one. In the past decade, Chinese auto has met ups and downs, and the reality has proved that only the insistence on "brand upwards" and "keeping on positive R&D" is the right direction that Chinese local auto brands should be heading toward. Entering all middle and high-end markets of severe standards, to some extent, is to exhibit one's competitiveness to all customers.

GS8 has successfully upgraded Chinese local brands and even "Made in China" to a new high level, which is not a result of inflated pricing and not of verbal boast, but of actual orders and real sales figures. In the price range of 160 to 250 thousand yuan, it has received 40 thousand orders within 3 months with a sales volume of 9418 per month. We cannot say that it will not be surpassed by newcomers, but at least it is unprecedented.

The representatives of "Made in China" are Huawei in the technology domain, and Gree and Haier, the leading enterprises in the household appliance industry. In order to complete the mapping of "Made in China", auto enterprises must be included. A nation's image of manufacturing industry can only be set up around the world with its auto enterprises to sprint at full speed and to break the tape. In addition to the British, American, German, Japanese and Korean brands, the world auto industry is also going to embrace Chinese brands which are rising up as represented by Trumpchi.

There is No Shortcut to Technological Innovation

Walking along the production line of Trumpchi, one may have an illusion of being in a science-fictional world: robots are waving their giant arms to make precise welding and assembling, unmanned carts are delivering all kinds of parts to their exact positions; empty auto bodies are entering from one end one by one, and brand new Trumpchi cars are coming out from the other end in succession…

The connotation of the word "Trumpchi" is explained by Zeng Qinghong, President of GAC, as being lucky and happy. He says: we want to convey luck and happiness to all of our customers by our self-own brand cars.

But it is not easy to realize that beautiful wish. "When Trumpchi was newly launched, my faith almost collapsed." Wu Song has always been in charge of the production and sales of Trumpchi products. When other GAC joint venture brands, such as GAC HONDA and GAC TOYOTA, were earning a lot of money for the company, the baby Trumpchi had been faced with huge deficits for several consecutive years. He was irritated at the market's innate distrust on the quality and performance of self–own brands. What really toasted him upside down was his colleagues' mocking as "You will be sent to work on Trumpchi if you do not work hard."

Faced with the huge pressure brought by the dominance of joint venture brands in the market, self–own brand cars were predestinated not be able to win a position in the domestic market which was the biggest in the world and was developing at a high speed? Under such condition, they initiatively lowered the production and sales target of Trumpchi, but they insisted on keeping high product quality. Zeng Qinghong said that quality was the best guarantee for the success of Trumpchi brand. There was no such a brand without quality. The first task of Trumpchi was to ensure its quality. He firmly believed that Trumpchi would succeed.

After years of efforts, overcoming the most difficult period for self–own brand autos to be accepted by the market, Trumpchi started to become more and more popular for its excellent quality and high performance–cost ratio. From January to October in 2016, the accumulated sales volume of the whole series of Trumpchi is 296 thousand,

The engine production line of Trumpchi.

increasing by 126% year on year. The total sales volume of this year was expected to surpass 360 thousand, which would rank Trumpchi among the tops of Chinese auto brands in terms of development speed and profit making level.

When GAC self-own brand autos were newly launched, nearly nobody, including insiders and ordinary consumers, had faith in them, because at that time, Trumpchi had no experts, no money and no technology. It was mocked as a "3 NOs" company. The most critical problem was that GAC lack of vehicle design and R&D abilities. How could a self-own brand be made without the ability of vehicle design?

But it is out of everyone's expectation that GAC should have built up an international advanced auto research institute by investing more than 10 billion yuan. The number of research personnel has increased from around 30 to more than 3000. Now in the institute, we can find a dozen advanced laboratories of vehicle, power assembly, and new energy, etc., a trial production factory covering welding, coating, final assembly and machining, and special trial runways for auto calibration. The institute is equipped with an ability of making R&D, trial production, and testing for vehicles and key parts. All those factors are providing Trumpchi with outpouring momentum for its development. "GAC Research Institute is able to develop five new auto types per year." said Zhang Fan, Vice President of GAC Research Institute.

Growing from zero vehicle developing ability to a current capacity of launching a batch of auto types, developing a batch, and reserving a batch, now GAC Research Institute has launched a series of auto types covering the whole range of auto products. "The success of GAC Research Institute and the improvement of self-own brand auto design ability indicate that there is no shortcut to technological innovation. We must walk forward step by step." says Zeng Qinghong.

Zeng Qinghong, General Manager of Guangzhou Automobile Group Co., Ltd.

"The development of self-own bran autos will not be roses all the way, but I always believe that in the future self-own brand autos will surely take the lead in China's auto market, and Chinese self-own brand autos will definitely become popular around the world." As the one who has witnessed and participated in the whole rising process of China's auto industry, Zeng Qinghon denotes that not only ordinary passenger vehicles and commercial vehicles but also new energy autos are promising.

There are always great expectations for new-energy autos, but the research and development path is very tortuous. "Our feelings are very complicated when we see little obvious advancements or face even dead ends after investing a huge amount of money." says, Zeng Qinghong. But he believes that new-energy autos can definitely be involved in the lives of thousands of families in the future as ordinary autos do for the moment.

The Story of the "R&D Foreign Brain" Marco

Marco Mario Gilardi's office is located in the GAC Research Institute at Hualong Town of Panyu Disctrict of Guangzhou. As the Chief Egineer, Marco has participated in the whole process of the development of GAC's first self–own brand car "Trumpchi", playing a very important role. Huang Xiangdong, Director of GD Automobile Engineering Association and former President of GAC Research Institute, describes that Marco's importance to the development of Trumpchi is like a leg to a table: "A table has four legs, and if one is missing, a trouble comes along that the table will not be able to stand up."

There are many other "foreign brains" like Marco in Guangdong Province. In recent years, priority is put on the foreign expert introduction which is part of the talent introduction project of Guangdong Province. According to the statistics reported by the Provincial Statistics Bureau, the number of foreign experts introduced into mainland China in 2014 and 2015 is respectively 132.1 thousand person–time and 129.9 thousand person–time, weighting 21.3% and 20.8% in the whole country. The number of hired foreign experts is ranking the first in China. These foreign experts contribute their powers to the innovation–motivated development of Guangdong with their enthusiasm and specialized knowledge.

At the beginning of "the 11th Five–Year Plan" period, Guangzhou proposed the plan of producing self–own brand autos. In July 2006, GAC built up the GAC Research Institute based on the former Guangzhou Automobile Technology Center, which was especially responsible for the development of Gaungzhou self–own brand autos. Huang Xiangdong, former professor of the South China University of Technology and Vice President of GAC, took up the post as the first president of the Institute.

Marco, Chief Engineer of GAC Vehicle Integration

The newly established GAC Research Institute had only four technology departments except three service departments. There were only a little more than 30 research personnel, most of whom were young people without experience. That made it very difficult to develop their self–own brand cars. So they considered the task of recruiting talents as their top priority. Just at that time, Huang Xiangdong met his old friend Marco who he had not seen for 25 years at Turin, Italy.

"I had met some people who came from Guangdong in a cooperation project of GAC and FIAT, and with closer observation, I found Huang Xiangdong!" when talking about their second encounter, Marco said it was a fortune.

In the 80s of the 20th century, Huang Xiangdong used to work in FIAT Research Center, when Marco was newly enrolled in FIAT after graduation. They worked in the same office. When they met again, Marco had been working in FIAT for nearly 30 years, while Huang Xiangdong had also been focusing on the auto industry, working as professor at SCUT, Vice Presindent of GAC, and then being designated to build up GAC Research Institute.

At that time, FIAT had business lines in China, and Marco often came to China on business trips. He had a very good impression on China. After Huang Xiangdong had described the ideas on developing self-own brand autos to him, he often came over to make "a cameo appearance", giving young researchers some technical guidance.

"GAC Research Institute was very small at that time, and they only rented one floor from SCUT as their office. Marco often came over to make 'guest guidance' totally out of his willing to help his old friend and former colleague." Huang Xiangdong has admired Marco's personal quality very much since he was working in Italy.

In December 2007 and April 2008, after several rounds of difficult negotiations and detail consultations, GAC and FIAT signed the technology transfer contracts of engine and of chassis platform. Marco was designated to the company, taking charge of the business with GAC. At that time, the idea of making self-own brand autos was quite clear and had entered actual preparation stage. They were in greater want of talents.

GAC-FIAT Viaggio

Huang Xiangdong considered directly hiring Marco to work in GAC.

"Are you willing to work in GAC?" Huang Xiangdong asked Marco, who replied him with his usual humor: "What took you so long to ask me this question since we have been cooperating with each other?"

Leaving FIAT where he had been working for 29 years and leaving his wife alone in Italy, Marco said he had "found passion and target here." Faced with Huang Xiangdong's invitation, Marco hesitated though he thought it might be a good idea. Marco had been working in FIAT for nearly 30 years, holding a relatively high post, and he should have been able to work until retirement without any big changes. And at that time his two daughters had grown up and were working overseas. If he also left, his wife would be left alone in Italy. It was not an easy decision for him to make. FIAT also tried to retain him. "Somebody told me that FIAT had already introduced Chrysler Company, and if you want to have some overseas working experience, you can go to Chrysler Company." Besides, compared with Chrysler, GAC at that time was only a small company which was little known internationally.

But Marco finally chose GAC, which was hard to understand for many people. But he described it as "a choice following his heart." "I suddenly realized that I had spent 29 years in FIAT and I did not want to continue." Marco thought that he needed a new challenge and a turning point. "It was not bad if I continued to work in FIAT routinely, but I always believed that I could also make a good career in China if I was good enough."

"I had a very good impression on GAC during previous cooperation, because I had found passion and target here." When talking about the choice he made at that time, Marco said that he was touched by GAC's atmosphere and the personnel's passion. "Having known about GAC's personnel, I increasingly found that the young people here had great enthusiasm to do it well. The management members here also had strong determination to establish the biggest and strongest leading enterprise in the auto industry. So I became more and more impressed and interested by the people and affairs here." Besides, Marco was well prepared because of the knowledge accumulated from his past working experience: "I wanted a chance to start from zero and to turn over a new page. But it was not a zero start in another sense, because I had acquired very good experience from the past."

Starting from nothing, not even chassis, GAC Research Institute developed its first self-own brand. Marco's importance was like an indispensable leg to a table. In November 2009, Marco joined GAC, when the working condition was still very poor, even the laboratory had not been built up yet, while the target of Guangzhou at that time was to

GAC Research Institute at Hualong Town, Panyu District, Guangzhou.

welcome guests by using Guangzhou self–own brand cars during the Asian Games which would be held in Guangzhou in 2010. Relevant Guangzhou government officers considered it as "the No.1 Self–Innovation Project of Guangzhou."

At first, many people thought it was a "mission impossible". After joining it, Marco started to lead the young team to set off toward the target. He was mainly responsible for the development of vehicle integration and chassis. In order to finish the tasks smoothly, Marco hardly took a rest even at weekends, and he also needed to make experiments outside Guangzhou. "We conducted vehicle experiment in Xiangyang, sand field experiment in Baotou, and ice and snow experiment in Heilong jiang."

Of course, all the members of his team worked at the same tempo. "Not only me who worked overtime at weekends, so did many team members. I worked, they worked. It was not me who was pushing them; instead it was them who were pushing me." It was of course not a small difficulty to develop the first self–own brand auto in two years. As Huang

Trumpchi assisted in Guangzhou Asian Games.

Xiangdong put it, they started from nothing, not even chassis. But, this team overcame many difficulties. In September 2010, eve of Guangzhou Asian Games, GAC's first self–own brand car "Trumpchi" finally came off the production line, realizing the "self–own brand auto dream" which Guangzhou people had been making for years.

As planned, 500 Trumpchi cars, as official automobiles for the 16th Asian Games, provided services to distinguished guests from Asia and all around the world. "Marco was involved in the whole process." said Huang Xiangdong.

"At the beginning, our team was very weak without any experience and was in want of someone to guide. At that critical moment, we needed backbones. And Marco was one. Huang Xiangdong says that when the team has grown up step by step, he is still needed as a backbone. "The whole team can perform well only when its core can perform well, and Marco is one of the most excellent members of the core team." In September 2014, the Chinese Government awarded Marco the highest honor for foreigners—the National "Friendship Award". In April 2015, Marco was successfully included in the fourth national "Recruitment Program of Thousand Foreign Experts". But, Marco does not consider himself as a "mentor". "I never teach them anything. I just work with them." says he.

Introducing foreign experts has become very common in Guangdong Province. According to the figure reported by GD Foreign Expert Bureau, in recent five years, the number of foreign experts coming to work in Guangdong exceeds 130 thousand person-times per year, which accounts for one fifth in China, ranking the first place. The accumulated number of introduced overseas talents is 37 thousand, among whom 129 are Nobel Prize winners, academicians from developed countries, and lifelong professors and 19 are included in the national "Recruitment Program of Thousand Foreign Experts". How can we make full use of these "foreign brains" and make them better service the innovation-motivated development of Guangdong? According to Huang Xiangdong, the first thing to consider is the outer atmosphere. We must provide them with privileged conditions. He thinks that we do not lack of privileged conditions either in Guangdong or in Guangzhou.

"But there are also many enterprises in which talents cannot perform well because they are not trusted in many cases." According to Huang Xiangdong, who has introduced many foreign experts, in order to make good use of "foreign brains", we must show our trust to those real talents when they have come here. We should provide them with a platform and entrust them with important post to make them perform steadily and in a long run. "Now in many enterprises, talents always leave short after being introduced. What is the reason? There must be a problem of corporation culture and trust. They do not feel happy working there, or they are not entrusted to do practical tasks."

"In addition, for example, high-level experts often get paid by a salary system different from ordinary employees. "If all the employees don't like the introduced talent and think that he performs worse than them but gets better paid, that is also a problem." In Huang Xiangdong's opinion, optimizing allocation is an art and a technique. "The key is how the main management members of the company treat talents, and how they really trust and cherish talents."

"The talent has both strong points and weak points. He is strong on one hand and weak on the other hand. We must tolerate his weakness and exploit his strengths. If we only want to take some advantages of him but do not trust him, we definitely cannot make full use of his talent." says Huang Xiangdong.

Guangdong "Unmanned Aerial Vehicle" is Flying over Global Sky

The Legend of EHANG as Entering Dubai

The news was quickly spreading on the front page of many mainstream media and was called by many people as "Guangdong's Pride". Dubai local media Arabian Business, by quoting the statements of Dubai Office of Transportation, reported on 13th February that "EHANG 182" was equipped with touch panels in front of customers' seats. The drone would fly to the preset destination where customers had selected on the map. The flight was actually monitored and controlled by the ground control center. Dubai Civil Aviation Administration had issued the test flight license. The UAE Telecommunication was responsible to provide 4G network for the communication between the drone and the ground control center.

On 14th, the British Media BBC, by quoting the opinion of Doctor Steve Wright who was an aviation expert from University of West of England, reported that before it could fly carrying passengers, the drone must pass an unmanned flight test for over 1000 hours.

The unmanned aerial vehicles from Gaungdong are showing the honor and dream of "flying over global sky". Following DJI's occupation of global consumer drone market, industrial application technology is also set off. In addition to EHANG passenger-carrying drones, Guangzhou Xaircraft Company is the first to set up affiliates in Japan, engaging in the domain of plant protection in Japan. Regardless of UAV toys, the overseas hot sales of drones can be deemed as an industrial success, an exportation of high value-added manufacturing industry.

In January 2016 in the U.S., "EHANG 184" was exhibited on the National Consumer Electronics Show for the first time. It was known as the first low altitude short-to-medium-distance automated passenger-carrying aircraft. "184" means 1 passenger, 8 propellers and 4 obtrusive arms. According to the introduction on EHANG official webpage, the 240 kg-net-weight "EHANG 184" is only electronically powered, which promises a 25-minute flight at sea level, with an average cruising speed of 60 km/h and a designed flying height up to 3500 meters over sea level. The drone's rated load is 100kg, with a trunk capable of holding an 18-inch luggage. Besides, "EHANG 184" is also equipped with an independent coding key to encrypt its communication systems.

Xiong Yifang, founder of EHANG

EHANG passenger-carrying drone

According to public information, Guangzhou EHANG was established by Hu Huazhi and Xiong Yifang in 2014. In December of the same year, it received an A-class financing of 10 million dollars from GGV Capital, then a B-class financing of 42 million dollars in August 2015. Now the company has around 300 personnel.

One is model airplane enthusiast and technology enthusiast, one has overseas study experience, and one is good at marketing. In 2014, three business starters encountered in Guangzhou, and then a drone company named EHANG was born in Tianhe District. From then on, this drone company which represents Guangzhou is developing extraordinarily.

In 2014, coming back to China to start up a business after graduation from Duke University in America, Xiong Yifang met Hu Huazhi in Beijing who was demonstrating the unmanned aerial vehicle to the investor. That was the year when unmanned aerial vehicles were springing up. The leading drone company DJI which was located in Shenzhen acquired nearly 70% share of the global commercial drone market. More and more companies started to enter the domain of unmanned aerial vehicles, among which the internet enterprises especially MI and TENCENT were reported many times to expand their business to make drones. But in Guangzhou at that time there were no drone companies.

When Xiong Yifang later got to know the sales talent Yang Zhenquan, the three chimed in easily. They developed products aiming at the automatic drone market. People can easily control the flight of drone by simply installing an APP in their cellphone, and they can also make the drone follow them automatically.

EHANG, riding on the wind of drone industry, was developing rapidly like a rocket shooting to the sky. It got a financing of 10 million dollars only half year after its establishment. Its estimated value had increased by 25 times within 6 months. And the company was assessed by the American magazine *Fast Company* as one of the top 50 most innovative companies in 2014, ranking the second. According to Yang Zhenquan, Guangzhou is an internationalized trading metropolis and a place where the regulations and supply chains are very suitable for making hardware. They are very thankful to this hot land of innovation and business venture, which nurtures EHANG to grow at a "flying" speed.

On the Lantern Festival in 2017, Guangzhou witnessed the creation of a romantic Guinness record at Hai Xinsha—1000 drones teamed up to make fancy performances, flying up to 100–meter height in the night sky scattering like thousands of dancing stars. They drew many excellent light paintings such as Golden Rooster Crowing, Welcoming New Year, and Beautiful Landscape of China, etc. A Guinness world record of "the largest UAV formation flight performance" was created. This "thousand drones

A thousand drones performing above the Pearl River.

changing" performance was provided by the Guangzhou Chi–Made Company of EHANG.

On the night of the Lantern Festival, when the clock hand pointed to 9, "Take off", at hearing the countdown voice from the interphone, 60 artists from Guangzhou Symphony Orchestra started to play the famous symphony *Yellow River·the Third Movement*, and 1000 intelligent aerial cameras GHOSTDRONE2 were rising slowly along with the music. In Huacheng Plaza which was on the opposite side of Haixinsha across the river, the crowded audience all raised their head staring at the most fantastic performance. Behind this performance, EHANG started to develop the drone formation performance technology two years ago. They decided to employ real–time communication network of UVA formation to ensure that the whole performance would not be affected even when single drone broke down or suffered from communication obstruction.

The most outstanding point of this Guinness record breaking was that only one person, one computer and one–key control were needed at the backstage. A technical person said that the UVA formation performance conducted at Guangzhou session of 2016 CCTV Spring Festival Party was actually controlled by many top players invited from around China by using remote controllers, in order to lower technical requirement and risk. Now in this performance there were 1000 drones. It was impossible to hire 1000 players to control them on site. Therefore, engineers designed a set of high efficient remote control system of UVA formation, which would simultaneously tell every aircraft how to fly, where to stay, how to change team pattern, and what light color to put on, etc.

In 2017, the "Circles of Friends" all around the world were occupied by all kinds of UAV formation flight performances. At this year's CCTV Spring Festival Party, the unmanned aerial vehicle appeared again. One type of pocket drones finished a highly difficult indoor–stage big formation flight in the show "City of Fireworks", which made it become the face

The performance site of "City of Fireworks".

and ability representative for science at that party. International technology companies all treat the unmanned aerial vehicle as a powerful weapon for them to conquer the entertainment industry and to build up a good brand image.

From the Guangzhou Session of 2016 CCTV Spring Festival Party when UAV formation flight performance became popular overnight, eve of last Summer Davos Forum ceremony when 36 drones were dancing in front of Klaus Schwab, founder and Chairman of the World Economic Forum, to the current Guinness record, they all signify Guangzhou's desire for building an "intelligence made" city with technological factors. China is the market where the UAV industry is growing most vigorously, and Guangzhou becomes the brightest stage of unmanned aerial vehicles for the moment.

Wang Tao: Unreasonably Enthusiastic about the Sky

In addition to Guangzhou EHANG, there is another UAV giant in Guangdong—Shenzhen DJI, whose products occupy nearly 70% share of global civil small drone markets. DJI focuses on markets in European countries, from which nearly 80% of its total past sales is gained. The first mega millionaire of global UAV industry is a Chinese named Wang Tao. By Forbes's definition, Wang Tao is the owner of DJI.

Now DJI can sell several hundred thousand unmanned aerial

Wang Tao, founder of DJI

Unmanned aerial vehicles at film shooting sites.

vehicles—most are its main type—the Phantom series. From 2009 to 2014, the sales revenue of DJI has been increasing by two to three times per year. In May 2015, DJI got an investment of 75 million dollars from Accel Partners, while the personal assets of Wang Tao, who own 45% of the company share, would reach at nearly 4 billion dollars.

The whole globe is paying attention to this company. Unmanned aerial vehicles are being used for commercial purpose at a large scale: UAVs transmitted real–time aerial images for Golden Globe Award; Rescue workers drew maps of disaster–affected areas depending on UAVs during the earthquake of magnitude 7.8 in Nepal; Farmers in Iowa use UAVs to monitor their cornfields; Facebook will provide wireless internet connection in African farming areas by using self–own UAV products; DJI unmanned aerial vehicles also appear at the shooting sites of *Game of Thrones* and the latest *Star Wars*.

On Wang Tao's office door there are two rows of Chinese characters—"Only bring your brain to work" and "Don't bring your emotions to work". The person in charge of DJI is following those rules. He is a leader whose languages are fierce but behaviors are quite rational.

He works more than 80 hours a week, with a single bed beside his desk.

Wang Tao was born in 1980. He got fascinated by the sky when he was a primary school boy. He started to become full of imagination about the sky after he had read a comic book telling a story about a red helicopter's adventures. At the age of sixteen, he got a high score in an exam, and his parents rewarded him with a remote-control helicopter that he had dreamed of for a long time. But, he broke that complicated thing before long, and did not receive the parts used for replacement from Hong Kong until several months later.

Since his academic performance was not so outstanding, his dream of getting admitted to the first-class American universities did not come

Phantom 4 Pro+ intelligent unmanned aerial cameras.

true. At that time, his favorite universities were MIT and Stanford, but after being rejected, he had to take the second best. He finally went to Hong Kong University of Science and Technology, majoring in electronic engineering. In the first three year of undergraduate study, Wang Tao always failed to find a target for his life. But in the fourth year when he developed a set of helicopter flight control systems, his life was changed.

It may be said that Wang Tao had sacrificed everything for the last group project. He even skipped classes and stayed up late till 5 o'clock in the morning. Though the hovering function of the airborne computer that he developed went wrong one night before when it should be shown in class, his efforts were not in vain. Li Zexiang, Professor of robot technology at HKUST, discovered Wang Tao's leadership talent and his comprehension ability of technology.

So, under his recommendation, this persistent student continued his study as a postgraduate. "I am not very clear whether Wang Tao is smarter than others." said Li Zexiang, "But, those who get high scores may not have excellent performance at work." Li Zexiang was DJI's adviser and investor at its early stage, and now is the chairman of the company board, owning 10% share.

At first, Wang Tao made prototypes of flight controller in university dormitory. In 2006, he, together with two classmates, came to China's manufacturing center—Shenzhen. They worked in an apartment with

DIY Drones is the gathering center for drone amateurs.

DJI flagship store in Seoul Korea.

three rooms. Wang Tao put all the rest of the scholarship he had won at university into the research and development. DJI sold to Chinese universities and state–own power companies 6000 dollars of parts, which were welded on the holders of their DIY drones.

As the core team had been established, Wang Tao continued product development and started to sell his products to foreign amateurs, who sent him e–mails from countries such as Germany and New Zealand. In America, Andrew, Chief Editor of Wired magazine, created the message board DIY Drones for drone amateurs, some of whom proposed that drone design should be transformed from single–rotor to quad–rotor because quad–rotor was cheaper and easier to program. DJI started to develop more advanced flight controllers equipped with automatic driving function. When the development was finished, Wang Tao brought them to some small trade shows for promotion, such as the Wireless Remote–Control Helicopter Assembly held in Mansi City, State of Indiana, in 2011.

By late 2012, DJI had owned all factors required for making a complete drone: software, propeller, holder, gimbals and remote controller. Finally, in January 2013, the company issued "Phantom", the first quad–

rotor aircraft which could take off at any time. It could fly within one hour after being unpacked, and it would not be dismantled at first falling. Thanks to its simplicity and usability, Phantom successfully broke into the non–professional drone market.

It is said that Wang Tao also needs to deal with all kinds of corporate spying. He asserted that the new drone companies emerging during last two years used to get DJI's designs illegally.

In recent years, DJI keeps expanding its overseas markets and has built up 70 offices step by step, stationing in all cities by light office mode. To be specific, there is sales and technical support in Japan, sales office in Korea, technical and logistics support in Germany and Holland, sales and marketing in Hollywood Northern America, research and development center in Palo Alto, and office in New York.

In overse as and even the whole global consumer markets of drones, DJI can be said to be of terminal dominance. From 2011 to 2015, its revenue was increasing by 3 to 5 times per year. According to statistics provided by DJI, its sales revenue in 2015 reached at 6 billion yuan. As the base was enlarged, the revenue growing speed slowed down in 2016, compared with that in 2015. The growth rate was around 60% to 70%. Calculated by 65%, DJI's revenue of last year was around 9.9 billion yuan.

Now more than 80% of DJI's revenue is gained from overseas, Northern America being the largest market followed by Europe. In 2016, the growth rate in Australia was relatively large.

The UAV: Transfigured into a Hard-working Farmer

Guangzhou XAIRCRAFT is another big name among the UAV brands in Guangdong. In XAIRCRAFT's eyes, the unmanned aerial vehicle is a hard-working farmer. She is entering the plant protection market in Japan, competing with Yamaha.

In November 2016, Yamaha's new UAV Fazer R was formally launched, at a sales price of 1.34244 million yen (that is 871.1 thousand yuan), equipped with a fuel injection engine of

Peng Bin, founder of XAIRCRAFT

20.6kW. Fazer R can spray pesticides to plants from the air, covering a farm area of nearly 4 hectares every time, and can carry 32 liter pesticides at most. In October of the same year, XAIRCRAFT also issued its latest P20 plant protection UVA and agricultural UVA flight control, and announced the launching of UAV sales and leasing business. It is known that the brand new P20 2017 plant protection UAV system includes drones, GNSS RTK positioning device (handheld mapping device, mobile base station, and fixed base station), A2 intelligent handheld terminator, pesticide box, injection machine, intelligent battery and charger. The system sells at 94999 yuan, while bare drone at 48500 yuan. And ordinary users can also choose to rent P20 plant protection UVAs by payment based on work volume.

XAIRCRAFT which was founded in 2007 has begun to develop plant protection UVA since 2012. It has made significant breakthroughs in agricultural UVA sector and has obtained many national and international technology patents. On 24th January, XAIRCRAFT announced the establishment of its Japanese affiliate and to formally stretch out the network of P20 plant protection UVA sales and plant protection service in Japan.

XAIRCRAFT UVAs are entering Japanese agricultural production sector.

According to Peng Bin who is the founder of XAIRCRAFT, through years of development in China, XAIRCRAFT has gained certain capacity in both technology and manufacture of agricultural UVAs, which has even reached certain advanced level. They choose to enter Japanese market because Japanese agriculture is facing the same problems as Chinese agriculture does, which are aging population, sharp increase of labor cost, and decrease of farming population, etc. But those problems occur in Japan much earlier than in China, which makes Japan be in stronger need of that kind of automatic agricultural UVAs.

As reported by the British *Financial Times*, few people outside Japan know that UVAs have been playing a very important role in Japanese farms since 1980s, when the motorcycle manufacturer Yamaha developed unmanned helicopters which were used to spray pesticides and to plant crops. On the dining–table of Japanese families, one in every two bowls of rice comes from the crops watered by Yamaha UVAs.

In the Chinese UVA sector, many companies choose to make multiple developments, while XAIRCRAFT chooses to focus on agriculture sector which is relatively less popular. Up to October 2016, Xplanet which is owned by XAIRCRAFT has established a service team of around 800 persons, covering a working area over 2 million hectares in 14 provinces around China and providing UVA plant protection services to nearly 100 thousand users. Besides, XAIRCRAFT has built up service headquarters in Xinjiang and He'nan.

"We have actually explored its applications in many sectors including logistics, public security, and the military, but in the process of final exploration we chose agriculture." Peng Bin says that agricultural market is broader, which can provide the companies like XAIRCRAFT with a better chance to exercise their abilities; secondly, there is much space in agriculture to be changed with technology, which is also the

XAIRCRAFT's original target that we wish to use our products or technology to solve certain technical problems.

There are four basic processes in agriculture. During the whole agricultural production cycle, ploughing, planting, managing and harvesting are the four basic factors, of which XAIRCRAFT participates in the managing process.

" XAIRCRAFT services farmers through two channels: the first one is XAIRCRAFT's self–run team, who can provide the government or big farmers with the spraying service, which is only charged against surface, for example, 10 or 15 yuan per hectare without buying UVAs; the second one is that XAIRCRAFT has many partners who can provide services to local farms and growers." says Peng Bin, "As rural lands are becoming more and more centralized and land transfer is becoming faster and faster, more and more farms will need such kind of services. In the future, agriculture will be a sector with finer and finer division of labor."

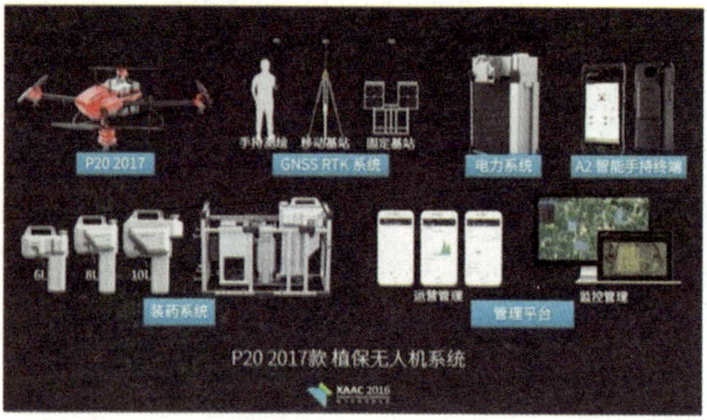

Plant protection UVA system

Guangdong College Startup Elites

Chen Di: A Company Carefully Advanced Step by Step against Incessant Occurrences

Chen Di, a graduate of class 2006 majoring in computer at South China University of Technology (hereinafter referred to as SCUT), was listed in "China's Top 30 Entrepreneurs under 30 Years Old" in the Chinese version of Forbes, who made such a comment on those listed entrepreneurs: "These young people who have shown their innovative ability in technology, product, and commercial mode have already acquired very powerful startup

UMI's business system diagram

Chen Di, founder of UMI

spirit and revolutionary capability."

According to the teachers and students of the School of Computer Science and Engineering at SCUT, Chen Di was a "technology enthusiast" and a "contest enthusiast". "I don't like doing written assignments, but it doesn't mean that I don't like study." Chen Di's passion for study was demonstrated not only by his enthusiasm for engaging in practices and experiments but also by his strong self-learning spirit. During the sophomore year, in order to join his senior schoolmate who had won a prize at the national challenge cup to develop a game, Chen Di, after finishing the classroom homework, stayed at the library to learn more computer technology knowledge until everyone had gone almost every day.

"SCUT's academic atmosphere was very free and open, and the school also encouraged us to do experiments. All those factors contributed a lot to my choice as to start up a business later on." Chen Di said, it was from the sophomore year that he started to participate in big contests such as "IBM Mainframe Application Innovation Contest", "Microsoft Elite Challenge", and "National Information Security Contest for College Students", etc. "The practical experiences with those famous enterprises in doing some practical training projects greatly contributed to my increasing hand-on ability." Chen Di is very grateful to his alma mater for providing him so many opportunities to exercise his knowledge. Those platforms not only taught him how to make project management and team cooperation but also guided him to try and to become sure about a suitable development direction. All that made a very good foundation for him to start up a business.

In fact, Chen Di who was born in Chaoshan had dreamed about becoming an entrepreneur since very young. Having participated in many contests and obtained some achievements, something called "innate commercial sensitivity" attacked his brain. He made repeated comparison and considerations, from big computers to PC markets. Based on his unconscious "commercial risk evaluation", he decided to start from mobile phone games.

"The young think it is a new market full of fun and chances." In the summer of 2007, Chen Di bought a cheap second-hand intelligent mobile phone from Zhonghua Plaza and started to program mobile applications with his classmates. When he realized how "cool" those mobile games could be, he organized a group of classmates who loved technology to form a workshop and started to make all kinds of mobile applications at the laboratory every day. Bluetooth Sanguo Kill, Bluetooth Doudizhu, 3D Table Tennis... were put on online for free download, and soon after, they were downloaded more than 2000 times per day. Before long, Chen Di's team was stuck in the dilemma of making charge or not. Faced with the inevitable conflict between developers and users, he said: "Some classmates enjoyed the pleasure of programming very much, but I prefered to transform technology into productivity. I would rather spend time to

The four co-founders of UMI from left to right: Cai Ruitao, Chen Di, Li Zhankeng, Ye Wensheng.

figure out how to commercialize a good product."

As a freshman, Chen Di made a website similar to Ctrip. But there were two problems: it was very hard and inefficient to sign contracts with merchants; it was very difficult to develop business since the website visitor volume was too low. Considering his major—computer, he learned the first startup lesson: he must develop core technology competitiveness.

In the sophomore year, Chen Di started to study technology entrepreneurship, and had basically formed a start-up team. After finishing the IBM mainframe project, he also wanted to establish a national credit system. But looking back, it was very difficult for a young start-up team to commercialize that project which was awarded as an excellent application but was not commercialized. He also participated in some contests organized by Microsoft, in which he was mainly required to develop some games and applications based on Microsoft frameworks. During the Olympic Games, Chen Di became an intern in Microsoft Beijing. He learned a lot there: "At that time I realized that PC startup era had gone."

In 2008, Chen Di's team participated in the National Information Security Contest for College Students held by Chengdu University of Electronic Science and Technology. They submitted a mobile application, the design principle of which was to record user's unlocking force so that other people could not open the phone even if they knew the code but typed it with a wrong force and tempo. The programming code was very simple and not long, but it was highly appraised and got awarded with the second prize. "It gave us a lot of confidence to start up a business aiming at mobile internet."

In 2010, the year of graduation, Chen Di was faced with three options: to pursuit postgraduate study as a recommended student, to participate in the exchange program in Singapore, or to start up a business on his own. The last one seemed to be the most "unreliable". His instructor wished him to grasp the opportunity of being recommended, and some team members were leaving to take internship in TENCENT. "Chen Di, you start up a business, we will stay with you; you pursuit your postgraduate study, we will still be with you!" When Chen Di was struggling with those options, two of his classmates who were also his core team members, Li Zhankeng and Zhang Nuanhui, firmly announced their "alliance determination" to him. Coincidently, many years later, that year is called by people as "the first year of mobile internet era".

On 1st April 2015, the fifth anniversary of UMI, Chen Di posted a speech video for celebrating the fifth anniversary of the advertising platform Youmi on its official website. Passionately he says that five years ago Youmi, the first mobile advertising platform in China, was established with a simple desire to make"all Chinese intelligent phone developers get paid". "The happiest thing is that we have helped nearly ten thousand advertising partners to promote their products such as APPs or mobile websites, and even have helped more than a hundred thousand independent developer partners to gain profit through advertising. At the same time, we have assisted more than one billion users around the world to get involved in the information dissemination in mobile internet through mobile advertising." Now, the start-up team has developed from a dozen people to more than 360 persons, from Guangzhou headquarter to affiliates in Beijing, Shanghai and Hong Kong, from Chinese market to international market! In the upcoming years, a close integration between the mobile internet and all kinds of sectors such as internet finance, O2O, intelligent hardware, healthcare, and education will become an outstanding light spot of this small era. UMI will actively participate in it, will continue to realize its value as a promoter for many products and services, and will help more developers, media and creators of new content to gain profit.

And he also stresses on connotation of UMI: "we have rice only when everybody has rice! "

Since 2015, UMI has been actively exercising its globalization strategies and has built up a global mobile advertising platform Adxmi which focuses on international business. Statistically speaking, Adxmi's advertising business covers double platforms—Android and IOS in Hong Kong, Macao, Taiwan, Southeast Asia (Thailand, Vietnam, Indonesia, the Philippines, Malaysia), Northern America, Southern America, and Europe,

The evolution of UMI Logo

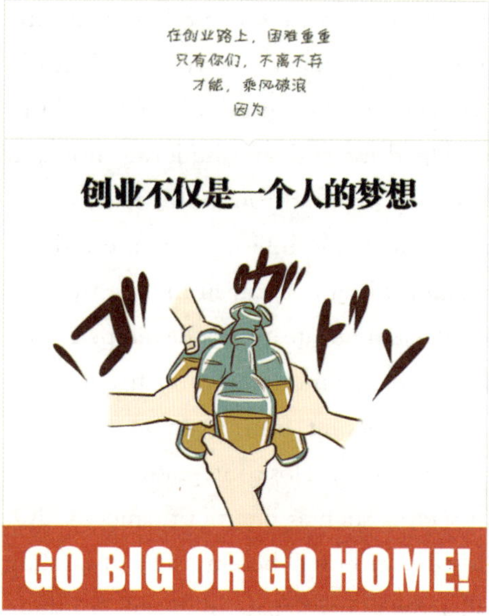

Cartoons of Chen Di's entrepreneurship on UMI website.

covering more than 200 districts and countries around the world and having strategic cooperation relations with 1500 medium channels in the world.

Mihui platform is another important chess that UMI has placed in its socialized marketing chessboard, following the APP advertising business "Youmi+Adxmi". It is designed to be a marketing platform focusing on socialized media. Now Mihui has accumulated more than 1000 opinion leaders, has cooperated with more than 100 thousand WeChat industrial official accounts, and has attracted more than 100 million fans.

So far, UMI has already made arrangements at all flow entrances of mobile internet, has gathered strong resources from all directions, and has built up a marketing ecosphere of mobile internet. According to accessible information, UMI's revenue scale, net profit, APP coverage scale, and terminal coverage volume are all ranking top in the sector. UMI is certain about its advantages of development in the long–tailed market. It has refused being acquired, insisting on developing independently, and determines to make the biggest independent mobile marketing platform in China.

In that year, UMI was selected as one of the 2015 Forbes China's Most Promising Unlisted Companies Top 10 and as 2015 China's Best Mobile Advertising Platform.

On 4th March 2016, UMI managed to get a financing of 250 million yuan at the New OTC (Over the Counter) Market, which renewed Chen Di's knowledge about the New OTC Market. He said that the whole financing process fully displayed the charm of the New OTC market. And the financing result was out of his expectation. The intended amount of funds was nearly 400 million, if at that time (when releasing the *Stock Issuance Plan*) we had not set the financing limit at 250 million or below, the financing amount might be bigger. Besides, the financing was very efficient that it only took one and a half months to get 250 million. The efficiency was increased a lot since we did not need to negotiate with VCs one by one.

As for future strategies, Chen Di describes a blueprint with "one horizontal line and several vertical lines": UMI takes the globalized mobile advertising platform as the "horizontal line" to expand its advertising business, and by taking advantages of the mobile advertising platform, it could focus on the "vertical lines" such as games, e–commercial, finance, education and O2O to deepen its business lines, gathering upstream and downstream of the sector and forming UMI's uniquely–own eco flow network. As for mobile advertising this "horizontal line" itself, Chen Di shows firm and strong confidence in the original intention of UMI's developing strategies: "At first our customers were mostly APP advertisers, now we have extended our business to over traditional brands promotion, websites promotion, and WeChat or market activities. Besides, developers have also made relevant extensions, from small APPs in the past, to now big APPs, and WeChat official accounts including 'we. Media' accounts, etc."

Wang Ruixu: a Post-90s CEO Who Made Proposals to the Premier

On the morning of 27th January 2015, in one meeting room at Zhongnanhai, Premier of the State Council, Li Keqiang was chairing a forum for the people of Science Education Culture and Health Care (SECH) and the grassroots representatives. Guided by the staff, Wang Ruixu, bringing a speech draft, a notebook and a pen with himself, arrived at one of the meeting rooms at Zhongnanhai. "Everyone's seat was arranged in advance, and there was a name list of speakers with speech order in front the seats."

Wang Ruixu said, he did not only noticed that he was the seventh to give a speech, but also that he was the only representative of Guangdong and also the youngest among the representatives participating in the forum. There were totally 10 persons, including himself, Yaoming, Chen Daoming, and Xu Ningsheng, etc.

"It was not until that moment that I completely understood the meeting content: Premier Li Keqiang would chair the forum and listen to the opinions and suggestions on the Government

Wang Ruixu, founder of JZM

Work Report (Exposure Draft) from the SECH people and the grassroots representatives." said Wang Ruixu.

"Soon after we had been seated, the Premier walked into the meeting room, smiling and holding hands with every present representative." said Wang Ruixu. Though he had practiced the scene a thousand times in mind, he still felt very nervous when he was truly holding Premier's hands and introducing himself to him. His hands were sweating during the whole process. "But I could still feel the Premier's affinity."

"When it was my turn, I had calmed down." Though he had prepared a speech draft, he finished his speech basically without turning to the draft. "It was mainly about proposals on college students' entrepreneurship by referring to my own experiences: I hoped the government to actually implement the supporting policies for college students' entrepreneurship and to create conditions for college entrepreneurs to realize their dreams."

"The Premier made an immediate response that college students are very important forces for promoting mass entrepreneurship and innovation. We must 'build up bridges and roads' and create conditions for them to realize their dreams and values." said Wang Ruixu.

Whereas on the evening of 6th Feburary, Wang Ruixu also forwarded a message titled as *Why Has Chen Daoming Been Invited by the Premier to Attend the Forum at Zhongnanhai* in his Circle of Friends, and left a message saying that "It was very happy to sit with Mr. Chen."

About 5 minutes after the CCTV News on the evening of 27th January, our customer service center received a call from one media requiring making an interview on us. In the next 20 minutes, we received interview appointment calls from a dozen media one after another." Ellen, who is working at Wang Ruixu's company in media promotion, says: "Nearly all media raised such a question to us: what makes Wang Ruixu the representative of post–90s entrepreneurs to participate in the Forum in Beijing?"

To that question, JZM start–up team gave a "powerful" response: he does not occupy the Circle of Friends, does not show his financing achievement in a high–profile manner, neither has he been reported on any gossips. Compared with those post–90s labels such as unscrupulousness, arrogance, and infantilism, people would prefer seeing other aspects of the post–90s, as being brave, persistent, practical and hard–working. And Wang Ruixu just happens to be a good example who insists on being the most hard–working and most persistent post–90s young entrepreneur."

Having participated in the Premier's Forum, Wang Ruixu became very popular. But his work was basically the same as usual, just as those things had never happened. On the morning of 29th January, he went to work as usual, and in the afternoon, he appeared in the 12th exchange meeting. He proposed suggestions on the establishment of one–stop service incubator base: "I hope that the incubator base can be made more of public welfare and of less commercial elements, and can provide one–stop supporting services including the service for college student's policy application."

Wang Ruixu has graduated from Guangzhou University of Chinese

Medicine for only half a year. Guangzhou Joiway Technology Ltd that he founded in the third year of his undergraduate study has successfully received a second round of Angel Investment and an A–class financing of tens of millions. The company is valued more than a hundred million yuan. But few people know that the young CEO today used to be an internet addicted teenager, who performed very well in both study and business in university after he had turned over a new leaf. From internet addicted teenager, college student entrepreneur, to the Premier's guest, his growth process is an "inspirational novel".

Indeed, Wang Ruixu has an extraordinary "resume": in addition to the 5 scholarships he won during his study at Guangzhou University of Chinese Medicine, he also won more than 30 prizes including the titles of "China's Excellent Volunteer of Science Popularization" and "Thousand Volunteer", the first prize of the first Guangzhou Creativity and

The young start-up team of JZM.

Entrepreneurship Contest for the Youth, the golden prize of Guangdong Entrepreneurship Practice “2014 Challenge Cup”, the first prize of the “Mobile Internet Design Contest of Guangdong, Hong Kong and Macau”, Medicated Diet Contest of Guangzhou University of Chinese Medicine, etc. And he also won each of the national and provincial training projects for entrepreneurship and innovation. He is a typical young entrepreneur who does well in both study and business.

His start–up experience is much more extraordinary. He started up a business in mobile APP, while he was majoring in a totally different area, the discipline of “Resources and Development of Chinese Medicine”. Before starting up a business, he used to work as security guard and to sell small goods on the street. He established the Modeng Team to make campus promotion for enterprises in the sophomore year. And in the third year, he founded the Joiway Technology with 70 thousand yuan he had saved, establishing a start–up team of 15 persons, which mainly focused on promoting “JZM” where college students could search for reliable part–time job information. He used to win the first “pot of gold” for starting up a business with a part–time job plan printed at 0.8 yuan.

It is out of imagination that Wang Ruixu used to be an “internet addicted teenager”. Wang Ruixu was born in Shantou, at a family which ran a wool factory. He started to assist his parents in handling the factory account when he was 11 years old. Since junior high school, Wang Ruixu started to visit the internet bar frequently, almost staying there several hours every day. “Once in order to pass an online game, during the whole 7–day May Day Holliday, me and my younger brother, we stayed all day long in the internet bar, taking turns in playing the game for 12 hours each one, and we even could not spare a time for eating.” recalled Wang Ruixu, before long, I became a definite problematic teenager who played online games, smoked, drunk, and skipped classes. It never rains but it pours. Before the senior high school entrance examination, his parents' factory was suddenly faced with crisis bearing a huge debt, and his family went bankrupt. Graduated from junior high school, Wang Ruixu handed to his mother an entrance examination sheet scoring 280. His mother slapped him heavily in the face. "My mother was crying. I could imagine how sad and helpless she was." Wang Ruixu was drawn back to the cruel reality, and he started to realize that he had to take on the heavy family responsibility.

So he proposed to take over his father's factory, which was however strongly against by his father. "He did not receive good education. So he did not want me to follow his old path." said Wang Ruixu.

Wang Ruixu was sent back to junior high school. His parents also ceased to let him study on his own, instead, they started to spend more time in monitoring his study. And in order to help him get rid of internet addiction, they intentionally sent him to a junior high school where there was no internet bar nearby.

Wang Ruixu got rid of internet addiction, studied very hard, got admitted by Shantou Overseas Chinese High School in the next year, and then was admitted by Guangzhou University of Chinese Medicine through the college entrance examination.

In the freshman year, he met his girlfriend. In order to maintain a relationship, he was always lack of money. Every time when he called for money, he could feel his mother's disappointment through the phone. His family was still in heavy debt due to bankruptcy. "I was macho as a typical Chaoshan man. I unconsciously wanted to protect my mother and did not want her to feel sad for me again". Wang Ruixu made a big determination as to earn money on his own. However, he, longing for a part−time job, was cheated by bad agents out of much money.

Wang Ruixu started up a business at Guangzhou University of

JZM's advertising page is colorful and lively, which goes well with young people's taste.

Chinese Medicine. He worked on a 1.5m–long and 0.6m–wide table, located in the east of the canteen, with a capacity of holding 4 persons. On this table, Wang Ruixu recruited his team members one by one. They formed the Modeng Team and worked hard for their business. "At that time, even a smile from a senior female worker in the canteen was a great encouragement for me."

From chagrin, discrimination, bitterness, persistence, and fighting, they gained the expansion of business, increasing number of team members from "song–and–dance duet" to "a choir of forty", and increase in revenue from zero to 150 thousand. It was also on that table that Wang Ruixu started to think about the future. Under the pressure of team development, and out of his unforgettable experience of college students part–time job market, Wang Ruixu founded the Joiway Technology Ltd and initiated the development of college students part–time job platform—the JZM. But at that time they had not enough money for the research and development. So except the technical, all the other team members engaged themselves again in campus agency and part–time jobs for a simplest purpose: to support the technical.

In 2013, he had owned a second table which was 2m in length and 0.8m in width, a phone, and a computer, and he worked with a group of like–minded young entrepreneurs.

It was located in a creative industry park in Baiyun District, a special free service area provided by Guangzhou Youth League for the youth to develop their business.

In the first Guangzhou Creativity and Entrepreneurship Contest for the Youth, the Youth League invited some experts and venture capitalists to "choose the horse". As an outstanding "dark horse",

Wang Ruixu was chosen. He did not only win the championship but also got a venture capital financing.

It was those painful experiences of being cheated when looking for part–time jobs that inspired Wang Ruixu to make "JZM". It was also because of that, he was very careful about the reliability of the posted information. In that contest, his "JZM" project did not only win the championship but also got a venture capital financing. Now, under Wang Ruixu's leadership, "JZM" has already attracted a million users and has successfully got a second round of Angel Investment and an A–class financing of ten millions. Faced with the problem of fierce internet "homogeneous competition", Wang Ruixu is very confident: "It will instead motivate our potentials to make this sector better."

He says that starting up a business is to make money, and as CEO, he has the responsibility to provide a better life to his team members. "So, starting up a business not making money is to behave like a hoodlum."

"As a grass–root post–90s from village, I cherish very much what I have now." Wang Ruixu uses his actions to bring new labels on the post–90s: brave, persistent, practical, and hard–working. At the beginning, as CEO of the team, Wang Ruixu had to take full charge of all affairs such as promotion, operation, and public relation. “My work was all-inclusive. I provided help anywhere I was needed. As the leader, I was obliged to provide guidance to others.” Now, as the responsibility division is becoming clearer and clearer and the team is getting bigger and bigger, Wang Ruixu is mainly in charge of coordinating the whole company.”

Wang Ruixu is working very hard, basically from 9 o’clock in the morning to 12 o’clock at night. “He seems able to do 10 persons’ work and often helps to do other work.” There was something wrong with his body when he was in Beijing, but on the next day Wang Ruixu insisted on going to work and attending the meeting at which he was invited. For that, his explanation is: “Now that I am an entrepreneur, I must learn to take on all the responsibilities brought by this identity. As for work, I am companied by my partners. I feel very good working hard together with them.”

Wang Ruixu indicates that as for activities related to entrepreneurship, once invited, he will always participate in them under general conditions. The Forum held on 27th January has brought more attention to Wang Ruixu. But for him and his team, only “behaving in low-profile and working in high-profile” is the unswerving principle. He keeps reminding his colleagues: keep working hard, never be cocky, and make good products steadfastly.

Pu Shaotao: Uremia Forced Me to Start up a Business

In the middle of May 2015, the fund account of South China University of Technology received 200 thousand yuan. The teacher was shocked by the donator's name—Pu Shaotao, a student of Grade 2005 who was diagnosed as having uremia and managed to finish his study with strong persistence, under the help of the university and its students. Since the maintenance treatment of his disease is costly, where is the 200 thousand yuan from?

In 2005, Pu Shaotao, from a village in Shanxi Province, was enrolled in South China University of Technology to become an honorable national defense student. Full of expectations for the future, he was diagnosed as having uremia in the end of 2006. Pu Shaotao did not complain nor blame on anyone; instead he chose to face the disease bravely. At that time, no matter he chose to accept renal transplantation or dialysis treatment, the costly medical treatment charge is unbearable both for him and his family from a remote village. Pu Shaotao had always been taking part-time jobs to support his life at university. He even seldom went home in order to reduce transportation expense. During his treatment in hospital, Pu Shaotao was optimistic and confident. To cooperate with the treatment, he insisted on drinking only one mouthful of water every day. He totally received a dozen dialysis treatments, which made him shake with great pain every time. But he never complained about it. Upon hearing the news, the teachers and students of South China University of Technology gathered a donation of more than 30 thousand yuan by the next day after he was sent to hospital. Later on, they organized several donations, charity performances and charity sales activities: some students sold their works of fine arts, some students donated half–year income gained from being private tutor, and some students organized charity performances, some students made a special website for him to report on his health condition and to ask for help... and the university also raised a love fund to help him.

After one year of treatment, he was basically getting well. After leaving the hospital, Pu Shaota came back to the university which provided him with a single dormitory. He insisted on making treatments four times a day, half an hour a time. Every day, the first thing he did after getting up was to make a dialysis treatment on his own before going to school. When he came back to the dormitory at noon, he continued to make another

Pu Shaotao

dialysis treatment, a third after class in the afternoon, and a fourth before going to bed at night. It was also himself who changed dressing for the wound, disinfected the room, and had injections and took pills on time.

The future looked dim, but Pu Shaotao never gave up. He always tried his best to do what he could. Due to his health condition, Pu Shaotao had to give up being a national defense student. Then he started to learn his favorite computer programming on his own. "I have to learn a professional skill." Pu Shaotao started to think for himself. So he took computer as a selective course, and also learned it from online courses.

If someone was passing Pu Shaotao's dormitory at that time, he would see him making treatment and typing the keyboard at the same time. "Time seemed to pass very fast when I was learning programming." said Pu Shaotao with a smile on his face, learning had also transferred his attention from the treatment pressure.

On one occasion, hearing the teacher say that he wanted the national student website be revised, Pu Shaotao recommended himself to take the job without a second thought. Now it only takes him one week to make a website. But it took him one month at that time since he was not skillful enough. "I summoned up courage and handed in the work", while the teacher thought that the new website was pretty good. Knowing that Pu Shaotao was able to design websites, teachers, with great passion, introduced new "clients" to him. During his study at university, Pu Shaotao designed websites for a dozen schools, and also got some orders outside school. The "part–time job" earned him some money to support his life, but more importantly, it gave him more confidence.

In 2007, Pu Shaotao was elected as the "Self–improvement Star of Chinese College Students" with a majority of votes.

In spite of the great honor he had gained, he was still faced with huge survival crisis. What Pu Shaotao expected for the future was to find a job to support himself. He never thought of starting up a business until he was faced with the embarrassment of "unemployment upon graduation".

In 2009, as a consequence of the finance crisis, graduates were faced with an unprecedentedly difficult job–hunting season. Nevertheless, quite a few good software development jobs were offered to Pu Shaotao because of his strong programming technique. Should I conceal the truth? Pu Shaotao struggled in mind, but he finally decided to tell the truth.

One company called him to register. He told them about his disease and assured them again and again that the disease would not affect his working performance and his health condition would not have anything to do with the company. But he was still rejected. "I understood the company." said Pu Shaotao with a sigh, "But I still felt quite disappointed when I heard other students talking about the jobs they had found." Till then, Pu Shaotao totally gave up hunting for a job.

Most people start up a business out of interest or for pursuing a dream, but Pu Shaotao chose to start up a business because he found no other way out. Just at that moment, the teacher delivered a piece of good news to him: the government was encouraging graduates to start their own business and the qualified graduates could get an initial fund. Therefore, Pu Shaota got 100 thousand yuan to start his business.

After graduation, in a rented house he shared with others, Pu Shaotao alone started the business of website design and maintenance. He was struggling in hesitation as whether he should make recruitment or not since he was short of money. "What if I cannot get orders to support my personnel?" But one can never succeed if he never takes the first step. At last, Pu Shaotao cut off all the means of retreat and recruited 4 employees. They moved into another house with a surface of 140 m^2. Bearing great pressure, he had to do many things in person, and his body suffered a lot. One night at 10 o'clock, he delivered panels to his client. Then he missed the last bus for going home. It was raining hard that night. He walked for half an hour, which resulted in leg cramp. "I often stayed up late at night for orders only worth a few hundred yuan." Pu Shaotao was working extremely hard because he had no way to retreat.

More than one year later, Pu Shaotao realized that he did not make any money after deducting employee's salary and other expenses. In 2011, at his elder brother's advice, he turned to e-commerce, and became the first merchant who engaged in online make-to-order and sales of building materials and household products at TMALL. For business development, he moved from Guangzhou to Qingyuan. He registered and founded Qingxin Leyou Household Product Co., Ltd., of which the warehouse has been expanded from around 200㎡ to more than 1000㎡. The company has developed into a specialized window track supplier.

There are more and more online stores of similar types, and price wars against them resulted in low profit. It is not good for the company's development in the long run. Pu Shaotao has made breakthroughs from marketing mode and service quality, wishing to be "the one and only". He has established an offline service network around China in more than 1000 cities. "From the first installer, Guangzhou, we founded others in Xinjiang and Tibet in half a year. Once you have placed an order, an installer would immediately go to your house to provide professional installation service."

Pu Shaotao has also developed an ERP system which is specialized in the management of customization orders. Earlier, by using the ordinary online store sales system, they had to make pricing adjustments manually by referring to a table every time when the client made one change. It was inefficient and error-prone. Now with the modified system, their work load is largely reduced: "The work that required 15 sales persons to finish now only requires 10 persons."

In order to provide clients with better services, the company proposed a "20–yuan Rule", i.e. if the client finds the product unsatisfactory (color difference for example), he will be compensated from several yuan to 20 yuan by the company. As a result, some clients may get a compensation of 20 yuan even if they have just bought a 10–yuan product.

High–quality products and good customer experience made Pu Shaotao's "Zhishang Household" flagship store become the first brand of curtain accessories at TMALL. Since 2012, "Zhishang Household" has been ranked as KA Merchant at TMALL. Products can be replicated, and services can be imitated. If a company looks for a long–term development and transformation, it is critical for it to hold the core technology. Now Pu Shaotao is turning to intelligent household products. He is trying to realize a mobile control of all electronic household products. Now the hardware equipment is being tested. He says: "If it works, the customer will be able to open the air conditioner and fill up the bathtub before he arrives at home. In his words, "it is like installing a brain in the current product."

When the company is on track, Pu Shaotao repays the society in a more practical way. In Qingyuan, which is located in Northern Guangdong Province, most of his employees are not very well educated, who are mostly only graduated from senior high school, but they can get paid with four or five thousand yuan per month on average, some who are hard–working may event get more than ten thousand yuan. "It is even not difficult for them to buy a house." The company arranges health examinations for employees and also provides bonus to reward the excellent employees. Besides, he will donate 1 ‰ of every online order amount to the children in impoverished mountainous areas to help them go to school. Pu Shao also wants to open online sales channels for the agricultural products from Shanxi villages, wishing farmers to earn more money.

When he had finally saved some money, Pu Shaotao silently transferred

200 thousand yuan to the fund account of South China University of Technology, wishing to help students with serious diseases. He says: "At my most difficult time, it was the university and the society who gave me great love and help. Now that I have gained some power, I want to pass on that love and help."

When Factories and Villages Encounter the Internet

Factories are Revitalized by Internet+! Culture+!

Upon hearing the broadcasting in factory, workers were going home from work. Some of them were riding a bicycle taking his wife with him to buy food at the market located in the factory. Some of them, holding a ceramic teacup in hand and wearing the factory uniform and white gloves, were getting ready to take their children home from the school located in the factory. That is the memory of the workers who worked in the old factory located in Guangzhou Industrial Revenue in the 80s of the 20th century.

The Wechat headquarter located in the internet+ textile machinery plant

The TIT Creative Industry Center where Wechat headquarter is located and which is very well-known in South China grows out of the former Guangzhou Textile Machinery Plant founded in 1956 which was the largest textile machinery plant in South China at that time.

Today, the transformed TIT Creative Industry Center shows both a sense of old factory's vicissitudes and a cold-fashion sense of modern architecture. Extending from the front entrance towards the inner Center, there are 10 rectangular panel walls lined from cold color tone to warm color tone, the middle parts of which are hollowed with mannequin poses of different characters. In the Center, there are 21 primitive industrial factory buildings, crisscrossed pipe networks, and peculiar sculptures and industrial machinery models, scattering among more than 300 towering trees. Thus a peculiarly unique office space is woven. On the red brick factory walls are printed frescoes and slogans of strong historical characteristics saying "Cultivate the labor, Labor the cultivated". Those old industrial prints bring people back to 30 years ago.

There are around a dozen textile companies in the Center. Other companies are of sectors including internet technology, entertainment and media, architecture design, and catering, etc. Among them, the most famous is TENCENT WeChat headquarter which moved in two years ago and now occupies more than 5 factory buildings.

Employees are having meetings in twos and threes in the cafe near the company, and programmers are crazily clicking the keyboard in front of the computer...such scenes are not rare at TIT. By contrast, clothing shops are much less crowed. Most of them are playing high-end roles, self-

The beautiful door decorations, traditional walls, and modern clothes in TIT Center bring out the best in each other.

positioning as "top" "customized" high–class clothing clubs, and selling clothes of approximately 800 to 2000 yuan.

Turning off from the Center, we enter the E–commerce Industrial Zone, where the historic memory of this city is hovering and where the magnificent second entrepreneurship history raises the curtain.

Haizhu District which is located at the south of Guangzhou's new central axis becomes the main "internet+" battle field, with an "e–commerce avenue of Guangzhou southern central axis" formed along the axis. Guang Yi International E–Commerce Industrial Park grows out of the former Guangzhou Diyi Pump Plant. The Park covers 38 thousand m^2 and is mainly built for holding excellent big enterprises' headquarters and for incubating excellent breeding enterprises. It is included in e–commerce relevant supporting preferential policies of Haizhu District, and is positioned as a national–class e–commerce pilot park of cultural and technological integration. Now there are 45 enterprises in residence and 19 enterprises under incubation.

Having grown out of such transformation mode, the Park not only preserves the "Guang Yi" brand and style but also becomes a trademark of the "suppress the second industry and develop the third industry" project of Haizhu District.

The rapidly developing Guang Yi E–Commerce Park is ambitious, planning to transform and build up creative office buildings covering 30000–50000㎡, to introduce 3–5 famous e–commerce pilot enterprises, to gather 100 medium and small e–commerce companies, to realize an annual productivity density of 100 thousand yuan/㎡, tax density of 5000 yuan/㎡ or above, total annual production value of enterprises in residence of more than 1 billion yuan, paying tax more than 150 million yuan, in three years. The operator "group of five industries" includes e–commerce, technology, creative industry park development, and professional

Bronze sculptures are made at TIT Creative Industry Center to revive the workshop scenes of the old days.

institution of operation. The relevant responsible person, Zhang Minxu says that in the process of upgrading the factory zone into an e–commerce zone, physical space is only a foundation, which provides headquarter and breeding enterprises with "catalysts" such as administrative support, start–up investment, industrial cooperation, and entrepreneurship atmosphere, and what is more important is to create the "chemical space" which makes enterprises succeed easily.

"For example, why would a company choose to place its office at the Park instead of in the office buildings at Tianhe North or Zhujiang New Town? The rent would be one factor, but employee's working status, creative space, and innovative communities are more important."

According to Zhang Minxu, the transformation of old factory into new e–commerce zone must be deeply rooted in the two big soils of local economic upgrades and urban upgrades, virtually realizing a transformation from "physical space" to "chemical space".

Culture+Museum is leading, and People's Printing House is designing the most advanced product

At the same time when the "suppress the second industry and develop the third industry" strategy is sweeping over Guangzhou, the creative industry is growing up. Old factory zones are being upgraded.

As "an art and living center defined by international standard", Redtory Art & Design Factory still preserves a strong factory style. Now, here we find galleries well–known both at home and abroad, design workshops, art display spaces, fashion shops, special restaurants and cafes. You can also feel young and fresh atmosphere brought by leisure art and entertainment. The young people who love culture and arts write passionately: "When you are alone, you will fall in love with this place."

In 1956, China's biggest can factory "Guangdong Can Plant" was born here. In 1994, it was renamed as "Guangzhou Ying Jing Qian Enterprise Group Company". As part of the "suppress the second industry and develop the third industry" project, "YIQ" moved out, and artists transformed the abandoned workshops into LOFT–style blocks.

Block–printed ancient paintings, bronze–type printed models, ink–printing equipment, salt–water –powered flashlight...the Guangzhou People's Printing House located in Yanzigang South Road is one of our memories along the Industrial Avenue. The printing production has been moved out from Haizhu District, while the old plant's brand stays. The factory has been quietly transformed into a "creative industrial park of packaging and printing culture", where we can find Guangzhou Printing Museum which tells us about the printing history, the Research and Development Center of Anti–forgery Technology, and the Research and Development Base of Industrial Packaging Design.

The 60–year old Guangzhou People's Printing House is quite familiar to many Guangzhou residents. The food coupons, oil coupons, bond coupons, tax coupons, and residence booklets were all printed there. Since a few years ago, the Printing House has already started to make transformation quietly. The main printing production has been moved out

The main entrance of Guang Yin Creative Industrial Park.

to Baiyun District, while the old factory in Haizhu has become the first creative industrial park of printing culture in Guangdong Province.

Walking into the Creative Industrial Park of Printing Culture, we are mostly attracted by the Printing History Museum. The 800-square meter museum, which used to be a warehouse for printing inks and papers, now displays the whole printing history in epitome from oracle bone inscriptions to the latest digital printing. There we can see not only many entities of block printing and type printing but also the live performance of engraving Buddhist scriptures printing which was the most popular in Tang Dynasty.

There are also many very old printing machines being exhibited, which are, according the Printing House's responsible person, left by the old printing house. Among them we find the ink printing equipment with which the older-generation people are familiar — letters were carved on a stencil paper, which was then brushed by a brush full of ink, which then printed the letters on papers. Those who were studying at primary school in 70s or 80s all have all done exam papers printed in that way. Now the Museum is applying for becoming an education base of patriotism and popular science.

On the second floor are exhibited the entities representing the latest modern industrial design concepts. One of the exhibited items is very interesting. With an injection of 300ml light salt water, the flashlight can work for 100 hours. "You can even inject sea water or urine. It is the first choice at emergency." The designer is displaying and introducing this patented salt–water flashlight at the same time. Once launched, it attracted a lot of orders from Japan and became a necessity of Japanese earthquake emergency kits.

Near to the Industrial Center of Packaging Design is situated the Research and Development Center of Anti–forgery Technology, which has developed a dozen anti–forgery technologies that have been applied in packaging designs. The worldwide famous HP Company has also established an exhibition center in the Creative Industrial Park.

The transformation of the Creative Industrial Park where the Printing Museum is located will be divided into three phases, covering 10800 m^2 with a total investment of 150 million yuan. In addition to the Printing Museum, there will also be High–tech R&D Area, Cultural Creation Design Area, Patented Technology Incubation Area, and Anti–forgery Technology Application Center, gathering a bunch of printing–related high–tech research and development companies, cultural creation companies, and packaging design companies.

The"factory museum" of old memories records the entrepreneurship history of Guangzhou

The rising of e–commerce centers and creative industry parks does not erase the glorious industrial development history of Guangzhou.

The 75–year old worker Mr. Huang often takes a walk in the Creative Park. He started to work in Guangzhou Textile Machinery Plant in 1968, when the factory buildings were surrounded by bamboos and seemed very

Factory buildings in the Dong Fang Hong Creative Industry Park are transformed into modern offices.

deserted. “Its best time was in the middle of the 90s, when there were more than 1300 workers, one general manager and nine deputy managers, who were called as “top 10 generals” by many workers for fun.”

More than half a century passing by, the heroes have turned from “plant generals” into creative talents. Mr. Huang is very satisfied: “I have not expected that most of the factory buildings are preserved after the plant was shut down. The factory building that was used by the supply department in which I was working now has become a hotel.”

Xiaoshang, a college student who is preparing for the IELTS examination at a continuation school nearby, is showing TIT to his friends who are from Beijing. His introduction is very simple but powerful: “This is Guangzhou’s version of 798 (a very famous creative park in Beijing).” At the north of the Creative Park, the construction of TIT Phase II is in full swing.

No. 313 Industry Avenue Middle, the three huge characters “Dong fanghong” written on the entrance door make people feel they were back to earlier ages. Dongfanghong Printing House was built in 1968. Since the 90s of 20th century, new printing houses were blooming. DFH was regarded as "the Whampoa Military Academy" in the printing sector, attracting many people to come to be apprentice. Later the House declined, and many private printing plants head hunted their technical personnel, who could easily pass the job interview without taking any examination as long as they were wearing DFH's uniform.

In 2009, DFH shut down the printing workshop and moved out from Guangzhou. Now "Dongfanghong" on the arched door is still shining but has become the brand of "Dongfanghong Creative Industry Park". The old factories are completely preserved with all kinds of slogans left on the brick walls. Now this area has already been occupied by photography studios, internet companies, and a "Research Institute of Brand Problems" which confuses most people...the old factory buildings are changed. There are no workers any more, but are the tourists who are attracted by its fame and models wearing peculiar clothes.

The glorious industry development history of Guangzhou arouses every visitor's feelings. The Xie Tong He Machine Plant, which was located on the west of White Goose Lake and by the side of Ming Ling Ancient Bridge, was fabulously well–known in Chinese history. In 1915, the first Chinese diesel engine was made there, which lifted a flag for Chinese modern national industry. After People's Republic of China was founded, it became part of Guangzhou Diesel Engine Plant. In 2011, that 100–year old factory was shut down and became a "Diesel Engine Museum", which displayed the historical working scenes of sweating workers taking the old machines as stage background.

Along with the development of industry and updates of technology, old production tools and materials are being constantly abandoned, those of which have been preserved contribute to today's "factory museum".

"Taobao" Shops are Flourishing at the Villages of Guangdong

Approaching 12 o'clock at night, it seems very quiet at Junpu Village, Jieyang City, Guangdong Province. Along the famous Intelligent Street of the village, most online wholesales shops have been closed. Peeping through the doors, you may see the packed clothes which are piled as a small mountain in some shops. As one of the most famous "Taobao" villages of Guangdong Province, Junpu village gained an online sales amount over 80 million yuan

Guangzhou Conghua E-commerce Industry Park and Alibaba District-level Service Center of "Rural Taobao".

during the online shopping carnival "Double Elevens" in 2006. The success of Jupu Village's e−commerce is a good example for building the Junpu commercial zone in the east of Guangdong Province. Its experiences of development are being widely copied by other villages and towns in Jieyang.

Orientation training assembly of village−level service station of "rural Taobao" held at Wuhua County of Jiedong District, covering only 0.53 square kilometers, with 490 households of more than 2800 villagers. There are more than 350 households of nearly 2000 villagers engaging in online sales activities, opening more than 3000 online shops of all types and more than 320 real online wholesales shops. Here, except kids and the aged, all villagers are doing e−commerce. Many housewives also start to open online shops after receiving the free e−commerce training offered by the government. Now few people know that Junpu Village used to be a "problematic village" suffering from severe social conflicts. Changes have been made since three years ago, when several young workers came back from Guangzhou and started their online shop business on Taobao. They were then followed by countless villagers. Then Junpu Village, as becoming more and more crowed and more and more famous, was certified by the e−commerce giant Alibaba as one of the 14 "Tabao Villages" around china.

Now the big Junpu e−commerce zone has been basically established. The Junpu e−commerce mode, as a replicable experience, has been promoted by Jieyang government to all the villages in this city.

Yes! Village, this word has never been so close to the internet! On 15th February 2017, China's Ministry of Commerce issued a report on the establishment status of national agricultural product market system: the turnover of China's agricultural product e−commerce is expected to reach over 220 billion yuan in 2016. It is a fertile new land for the "villagers" of

Junpu Village is located at Xichang Town in the east.

Guangdong. At the ends of the hot "agricultural e-commerce" network, more and more rural small shops are becoming village-level service stations for e-commerce enterprises, playing an important role of sending, receiving, and transmitting express packages.

"I have to handle at least a dozen packages per day." Zhou Tingting who is the shop owner of a village-level service station at the Taiping Town of Shixing County of Shaoguang City of Guangdong which is jointed to that network tells the media happily. She says, now the online shopping packages are mainly household appliances, clothes and daily necessities, which can be delivered by electronic tricycle. The logistics pressure is not great, and she can earn a commission of two to three thousand yuan per month.

In 2006, Guangdong set a target that by 2020, the rural e-commerce application level around the whole province is obviously increased, the supporting service system of rural e-commerce is basically established, the double-flow channel of urban and rural products is basically formed, the scale of agricultural products online sales and rural online shopping continues to expand, and the whole development level ranks top in the whole China. There will be 50 county-level e-commerce industrial parks

Crippled Zhou Tingting at the village Tabao service station.

and 100 town-level e-commerce operational centers built up around the whole province, realizing a full coverage of rural e-commerce service station in all administrative villages. Relying on e-commerce, information technology, and logistics network, based on the "project of hundreds of thousands of rural markets", we should speed up the establishment of modern circulation network in rural area, and strengthen the service network, facility construction, and their connection of systematic logistics such as trading, sales and supply, and postal service, in order to facilitate the distribution of daily necessities to villages.

The college students, who are from rural areas and are admitted by urban colleges, are also trying their best to get villagers involved in sharing the internet bonus. Yuan Senlin, a rural student of Jinan University, heard a small story when he was conducting research in Xingning Meizhou during the sophomore summer holidays: a son who was working in Donguang sent some rice dumplings that were distributed by his company to his old father by express, but since the logistics service in rural area was under development and his father was not used to receive mails, that "fast delivery" became a "slow delivery", and the rice dumplings that were full of the son's love had become decay and uneatable when they were finally passed to the father's hands.

Yuan Senlin and other four "post–90s" who grew up in the same village and were studying in the city formed a team to start a project to build up a "rural–urban circulation" platform. The five young people were concerned about the same problem that since rural logistics and e–commerce were under development, it was difficult to deliver rural products to urban areas, and vice versa. The team he led hoped to build up a physical link to couple rural people and urban people by providing e–commerce services to farmers. Combining the research result and what they had learned, they divided the "rural–urban circulation" services into two sections, i.e., rural–urban logistics agency and online purchasing agency: as for logistics, they planned to set up warehouse headquarters in counties as gathering points of packages and to cooperate with convenience stores which would act as distribution stations from which customers get

The group photo of "rural-urban circulation" team members.

the package on their own; as for purchasing agency, they had developed shopping guide platforms to help farmers to make "online shopping".

This small team started to prepare for the "Challenge Cup" National Contest of College Students Entrepreneurship which would be held in New Year. In two years' time, from project to participation, the "rural-urban" team had traveled through more than 20 villages and towns in Guangdong Province to conduct research. In one village of Shanwei City, the students met an old man whose daughter was out to work all year round. He had planted longan trees in the field. But since the purchasing price was low and he was too old, most of the longans were left on the trees and became decay. Upon the old man's consent, the team led by Yuan Senlin picked 100 kg longans and brought them back to Shenzhen to sell online. The 100 kg fresh longans were quickly sold out in 50 minutes.

"The 'longan' sales event represented a problem that Chinese rural areas were commonly faced with: it was hard to deliver high-quality agricultural products to urban areas. It did not only affect farmers' income but would also result in resource waste. The 'rural-urban circulation' plan was to solve the problem of 'exportation' and 'delivery'." Then, the express industry which played the central role in transmission became the focus of the "rural-urban circulation" team's research program...

Thus, the "rural-urban circulation" model was being modified again and again based on their careful researches. When they were participating in the contest in Wuhan, one judge made a comment excitedly after hearing their speech. They were finally awarded the national golden prize of the contest.

Of course, there are many other people who are optimistic about the future of Guangdong rural e-commerce. "The rural e-commerce is a very promising." Chen Haiquan, Dean of Guangdong Research Institute of Asia-Pacific E-commerce, makes such comment in front of the media. He says, Guangdong rural e–commerce turnover is conservatively estimated to reach 28 billion in 2017, 43 billion by 2020. There are many special agricultural products in Guangdong. Special agriculture–related industries covering flowers and plants, fruits, sea food, and meat have been established in about 85% of the counties around the whole province. And Guangdong is not only a place which produce a large quantity of agricultural products but also an important consuming and gathering place for the agricultural products coming from places outside Guangdong Province.

The Internet Dreams of Urban Villages

On 23rd September 2016, Chinese Youth's Entrepreneurship and Employment Foundation signed a strategic cooperation framework agreement with Tianhe District Government of Guangzhou to build Chinese youth's entrepreneurship communities varying from 5000 to 30000 square meters in each of the 21 sub-districts of Tianhe District. It also means that the first Chinese youth's entrepreneurship community "5ipark" in the province will be located in the Tianhe District of Guangzhou.

The youth's internet entrepreneurship community "5ipark" is an internet incubation brand which is established by Wuxing Incubator Group, IDG Capital, and Chinese Youth's Entrepreneurship and Employment Foundation. There are plenty of reasons for her sturdy choice of locating in Guangdong.

Chen Zongxiong, Secretary of Chinese Youth's Entrepreneurship and Employment Foundation of the Central Committee of the Communist Youth League, is ambitious: "This is the first cooperative project of Chinese youth's entrepreneurship community made by the district administrative. I hope it can become a national example of district administrative cooperation in Tianhe and can be replicated and promoted." He says, Chinese youth's entrepreneurship community will become an integrated base for entrepreneurship contests, entrepreneurship training, entrepreneurship services, entrepreneurship finance, entrepreneurship social communication, entrepreneurship promotion, and entrepreneurship credit investigation, acting as a start-up "micro city" of working, living, and entertaining for young entrepreneurs. Guangdong Province is chosen as its first location and Tianhe District as its first station because Tianhe District has pioneering advantages in the IT and internet industry in China. At the same time, the Tianhe District Government has always been working on the construction of incubators in urban villages and plans to transform about 4 million m^2 urban real estates into public entrepreneurship space.

According to the agreement, both parties jointly promote and implement the project of "Chinese youth's entrepreneurship community and the sub-brand 5ipark youth's internet entrepreneurship community", initiating and creating a model developing mode as "one sub-district one community", i.e., trying to establish youth's entrepreneurship communities varying from 5000 to 30000 square meters in every sub-district, so as to form a service system of youth's double entrepreneurship incubation and to establish a talent base of youth's innovation and entrepreneurship, which can provide integrated resources for incubation and generate scale effects by making the start-up enterprises of different sub-districts be uniquely particular and complementary to each other.

In addition, in every youth's entrepreneurship community there will be a public space which will provide the young entrepreneurs with free stations and basic incubation services. They will try their best to realize 3000 free stations in Tianhe District in 2 years. Both parties will also found the Tianhe Sub–foundation of Chinese Youth's Entrepreneurship Foundation to provide special investment for the projects and teams that choose to locate in the youth's entrepreneurship community.

The 5ipark youth's entrepreneurship community is a model built in Tianhe District, which will be a comprehensive incubator covering 5i innovation factories, 5i incubators, 5i accelerators, 5i entrepreneurship apartments, and 5i creation streets." Zhang Minxu, co–founder of 5ipark Youth's Internet Entrepreneurship Community, said, 5ipark would create a multidimensional community cultural system of variant community combinations, diversified urban new spaces, regional or industrial activities of great influence power, specialized enrollment evaluations and community member services, and transplantations of trans–regional or trans–industrial resources. "It is not only to build up a fresh and new community space, but what is more important is to work with the enterprises and people in residence to form a more advanced urban working and living mode." explained Zhang Minxu, "5 ipark community is a prevailing public entrepreneurship space, an iterative product of start–up space, and an innovative incubator."

In the cities located in southern Guangdong, urban villages are inspired with stronger and stronger new entrepreneurship dreams. The Tangxia Street located in Zhongshan Avenue West of Guangzhou is a typical street of urban villages. An area of 7.42 square kilometers is shared by two urban villages, Tangxia and Tangdong, where live 350 thousand residents, among whom 260 thousand are migrant workers. The number of migrant workers in those two villages is so huge that it can rank top among that of all urban villages in Tianhe District. And they produce 230 tons of rubbish per day, which is one–sixth of the total rubbish produced in Tianhe District. Similar to most of the urban villages in Guangzhou, Tangixa Street's roads are narrow, rugged, covered with scattering rubbish at every corner, and crossed by numerous electric wires.

In order to make sure that incubators can also be located here, the Street dismantled many escalators and iron stands that are blocking the roads, expanded and newly built asphalt roads nearly 3500 meters, built up pavements 3000 meters, installed traffic bars 4200 meters, unblocked and newly built 150 sewers, and fixed 26 flood points. After that, the "micro recycling" management mode was introduced: four closed–off managed auto roads enabled an orderly circulation of automobiles in the village, 500 HD cameras were installed...the orderly construction helped to increase the rent of local real estates by 30% and attracted a bunch of high–tech enterprises which had great market potentials and strong innovative abilities to become residents there. In 3 months' time, Tangxia Street concentrated on renovating the surrounding environment of the village company's real estates, and then a New OTC Market incubator of certain scale was established in its old factory area.

The construction of "public entrepreneurship space in urban villages" is still an ongoing event in Tianhe. One third of the 11–milion–㎡ collective real estates of urban villages will be transformed into cost–efficient and novel–designed innovative development space. The innovative fusion of urban villages is taking effects. Tianhe District is opening its arms to numerous innovators and entrepreneurs by using relatively low cost and with comprehensive new service chains of innovation and entrepreneurship. At the same time, the urban villagers in Tianhe, who used to make a living by leasing their real estates, are jointing in the new economic trend. Some village collective economic organizations are even involved in investing in the internet ecologic home project, becoming part of the global innovation chain.

一只改变世界的企鹅

马化腾的三次危机

1987年9月，德国教授措恩在北京出席一个科技研讨会。经过一番调试后，他将北京的计算机应用技术研究所和卡尔斯鲁厄大学计算机中心实现了计算机联结。

9月14日，措恩与中国的王运丰教授共同起草了一封电子邮件，写道："Across the Great Wall we can reach every corner in the world."（越过长城，我们可以到达世界的每一个角落。）"This is the First Electronic Mail from China to Germany."（这是第一封中国到德国的电子邮件。）内容和标题均由英、德双语写成，也就是后来知名的"越过长城，走向世界"的邮件。在该邮件上署名的除了王运丰、措恩教授，还有11个中德双方的参与工作的人员。

但CSNET邮件服务器上却存在着一个问题——PMDF协议中一个漏洞导致了死循环，导致这个邮件的成功发出被延迟。经过咨询并得到了CSNET信息中心的确认：这个问题一直存在，尤其是在电话线路不好的时候。措恩教授的助手迈克尔·芬肯（Michael Finken）在北京与留守卡尔斯鲁厄的格德·威克（Gerd Wacker）共同努力，克服工作时差等多方障碍，用软件弥补了线路不稳造成的信号混乱。9月20日，这封邮件终于穿越了半个地球到达德国。

到了今天，45岁的广东汕头人马化腾创办腾讯整整18年了。刚刚过去几个月的2016年11月11日，是腾讯18周年纪念日，当天马化腾联合总裁办成员给在职员工、离职员工、外包人员和公司服务人员发出了总计3000万元的微信红包。

这并不是高潮。因为马化腾晚些时候还宣布了一个决定，给在职员工每人300股腾讯股票。按照其时腾讯每股200元港币的股价，他们预计拿出了15亿元用作此次奖励。

当然，腾讯的股价又是一个神话般的传奇。2004年6月16日，腾讯控股正式挂牌上市，当日以4.375港元开盘。12年后，这个价格累计涨幅超过了250倍。

随着移动终端的手机的发展，中国成为全世界互联网包括移动互联网最普及的国家。在马化腾的概念中，腾讯在过去5年里，从封闭的环境变成一个开放的环境，变成一个真正互联的生态。“内部的一些原有的业务做得不好的砍掉、卖掉、送出去，只保留最核心的通信和数字内容，包括现在提倡的——‘互联网+’，所谓的‘+’就是跟其他企业的充分合作。”

按照2300多亿美元的市值，腾讯已经是亚洲最大的互联网公司。这个自称是典型的“程序猿”、原本没打算开公司的企业家，在很多场合都表现得十分谦逊，面对自己人也不例外，“腾讯18年来，我更多讲的是感恩，感恩所有的同事们。”

实际上，他正手握一个极其惊人的用户群体和一个庞大的商业帝国。腾讯旗下微信和QQ的月活跃用户数已经分别达到8.06亿和8.99亿。2016年，中国大陆总人口也不过13亿8271万人。

他的形象儒雅白净，且外表温和，但这位“QQ之父”一直有很强的开拓力，以及伴随而来的很深的危机感。媒体评价他18年来的创业路径时，必然绕不开敬畏、创新、开放等几个关键词。

马化腾说，腾讯发展历程中遇到了最大的三次困难。

第一次是初期融资期，在发展初期团队投标失败、用户疯长，没钱买服务器，这是最难的时候。但这种困难也迫使腾讯团队从很早就想怎样有造血的能力。

第二次是跟MSN竞争。“别人都认为你死定了，只是什么时候死而已。最后还是挺住了，我们的产品做得比国外的产品更适合中国人使用。”能赢得与MSN之战主要在于QQ结合中国的网络环境和中国用户的使用习惯，做了很多优化。

第三个坎是五年前微信诞生之前，新浪微博从社交媒体转向社交网络，带来了很大压力。

当然，腾讯历史上最大的危机应该是“3Q大战”。奇虎360与腾讯间的纠葛由来已久，源于2010年双方“明星产品”之间的“互掐”。2010年9月27日，360发布了其新开发的“隐私保护器”，专门搜集QQ软件是否侵犯用户隐私。随后，QQ立即指出360浏览器涉嫌借黄色网站推广。2010年11月3日，腾讯宣布在装有360软件的电脑上停止运行QQ软件，用户必须卸载360软件才可登录QQ，强迫用户“二选一”。

为了各自的利益，从2010年到2014年，两家公司上演了一系列互联网之战，并走上了诉讼之路。

双方互诉三场，奇虎360败诉。其中奇虎360诉腾讯公司垄断案尤为引人注目，2014年10月16日上午，最高人民法院判定：认定腾讯旗下的QQ并不具备市场支配地位，驳回奇虎360的上诉，维持一审法院判决。

马化腾在当年的12月5日宣布腾讯进入为期半年的战略转型筹备期。他说，“垄断”是一个令人烦恼的罪名。在很多情况下这是一个假想敌，是一个不存在的东西。回顾20世纪90年代，大家看我们IT产业，微软是给人诟病最多的被指责垄断的公司。在互联网时代到来的时候，微软面临什么问题呢？我们看到很多新的公司照样可以崛起。几乎不可能所有创新者、创业者都认为毫无希望，微软可能进入很多领域，把很多产业都占到第一位的时候，那还有什么机会呢？我们看到，未来发展其实大家都有目共睹，不仅产生了Google，还产生了eBay，而且像Google这么强大的公司，已经无所不能，所有互联网产品线都有他的投入。我们看到仍然有Facebook的崛起，Facebook之后当人们觉得社交网站在人际关系上已经没有办法能够挑战他地位的时候，我们又看到一种新的形态，微博的形态崛起。

马化腾有点委屈地说，“所以，我们看到很多所谓的垄断，实际上在产业不断变革的时候，他依然面临很大的危机。也就是说，在价值变迁迅速的产业里面，没有一个公司是可以高枕无忧的。所以说，挑战像阿里巴巴、百度和腾讯——有人说是三座大山，有效方法不是建立一个类似的平台，形成一个垄断，而能够顺应而上形成一个好的产业链才是一个好的方法。”

“事后回想其实有很多的反思在这里面，但是我不想沉浸在所有的纷争之中，我更希望往前走，向前看。”马化腾说，这个纷争更加坚定了腾讯去改革，去转型的一个步伐。“我们希望这是一次慎重、彻底、完整的转型。”

此后，腾讯相继把搜索、电商等业务以投资的形式出让，专注做互联网公共事业的基础连接服务。

从模仿，到公敌，再到大哥的奇妙路径

IT评论人士评价腾讯的发展路径时说，“腾讯创办18年，走了一条从模仿，到公敌，再到大哥的奇妙路径。”

1984年，马化腾随父母来到深圳这座城市，从初中到大学都在深圳读书，毕业后在深圳的一家通信企业工作了六年，开始和初中、大学同班同学，还有一位电信行业的同行，总共五个人一起创业。当时全中国网民才300万人。

在1999年那时，互联网的发展究竟能给人带来多大的想象，恐怕并没有几个人可以站出来打包票。在整个互联网发展初期，很多时候互联网都是被作为技术去应用，很少有人去接触到。这样一种存在于技术层面的东西，很难给人一个想象空间。在这种大背景下，马化腾能够毅然决然地在买房和创业这个抉择上，发现互联网，并且做出了QQ，这显然是因为马化腾本身对于互联网和IM（即时通信）具有前瞻性——现在的雷布斯当年甚至也拒绝了对腾讯的投资。

你可以说，马化腾做QQ也是出于偶然——做电信相关产品开发的附属品，但是这显然不能够解释为什么QQ能够在接下来很短的时间内超越OICQ——当时IM的王牌产品。服务器存储、个性头像等等，这些现在我们看起来很普通的产品，在当时的意义可以说是不亚于现在微信的伟大创新。

再早一点，或者再晚一点，或许QQ都不会获得成功。正是抓住了中国互联网刚刚起步的第一波红利，QQ为之后的腾讯上市，乃至现在的社交帝国打下了坚实的基础。

腾讯在创业前阶段，准确抓住了几个重要关头。

首先是运营商的红利。QQ虽然在起步阶段就获得了大量用户，但是如何赚钱在当时显然是一个大问题。要知道，当时资本市场对互联网还是处于非常保守的状态，也没有现在的什么市梦率这一说，融资的击鼓传花产业链并没有成熟，企业更没有说“现阶段不考虑赢利”的底气。这时候，QQ抓住了运营商这根救命稻草，顺势进行了转身。

在当时，SP（服务提供商）类业务可以说是最早的互联网企业赚钱的方式。这对于QQ来说，算是救了QQ的命，如果没有这些SP业务，QQ或许真的会以100万元被卖掉也未可知。这些收入，不仅让QQ能够维持自己的运营，同时也为之后的上市打下了基础——在当时，互联网企业还是很难在不赢利的状态下就顺利让资本埋单的。在做SP的同时，QQ自身也相对比较争气。一方面在产品上接连推出了会员、QQ秀等具备增值收费能力的功能；另一方面也开始发行Q币，这可是到现在为止，唯一可以跟电话卡媲美的硬通货。尽管SP业务最终还是下滑了，但是QQ在这一波上，抓住了关键，让自己摆脱了困局。

其次是PC（个人计算机）应用的爆发期。在2005年，也就是腾讯上市之后，QQ几乎已经成为巨无霸型的产品。而在当时，正是桌面软件的爆发期，什么千千静听、暴风影音、迅雷、输入法等等，当时都会被软件市场列为装机必备。腾讯在这个时候，利用QQ的强大资源导流，开始向同类型的产品进军，先后出了类似于QQ影音、QQ音乐、QQ浏览器、QQ输入法等一系列的产品。尽管在当时遭到了行业的集体吐槽——血轮眼，但从现在来看，腾讯的很多横向拓展的产品，都是在这一波打下了基础。比如刚刚独立出来的QQ音乐，以及市场占有率已经排名前几位的QQ浏览器，等等。除此之外，QQ在这个时期也打败了MSN，可能很多人不知道，在MSN的巅峰时期，其市场占有率是超过QQ的。

腾讯还顺势一起推出了门户网站，在当时三大门户林立的状况下，生生靠着QQ的资源——mini弹窗、tips等等杀出了一条血路，最终和新浪、搜狐、网易并称为四大门户。这对于腾讯来说可是有战略意义的，除了由此可以掌握一定的话语权之外，还为之后的腾讯视频、腾讯体育等等打下了基础，门户的广告营收在当时对互联网企业来说是仅次于增值服务的重要营收。QQ在这个时期内打下的基础，既为自己之后的发展提供了空间，同时也是进行了战略性的防御。

再次是游戏的窗口。陈天桥的盛大将互联网拉入了“挖土机掘金”的时代，互联网企业在增值服务和广告之后，终于又找到了一个最快也是最大化的赚钱模式。腾讯很幸运地抓住了这个机会，这不仅是当时，更是现在的最重要营收，没有之一。在当时，腾讯进入游戏领域其实并没有那么顺利，前期代理的几个游戏都没有能够闯出来，甚至默默无闻，直到腾讯发现了棋牌类游戏，这个由腾讯自主研发的平台，在当时迅速打败了联众成为最热也是最火的平台。在这里，QQ的社交关系链真正有了用武之地，也是从此开始，腾讯意识到了社交和游戏具有天然的匹配度。在棋牌类游戏成功之后，腾讯推出的一些游戏类似于DNF和后来的CF等等，就开始接连成功，一直到现在的LOL，长期霸占着整个游戏市场的半壁江山。

最重要的是，腾讯抓住了社交网络的爆发期。Facebook的横空出世给了很多互联网公司启发，包括当时的校内网、开心网等一批网站都迅速发展了起来。在当时，这些网站的社交属性几乎可以跟QQ媲美，一时瑜亮。但QQ当时有一个最主要的撒手锏——QQ空间。据有关数据，在人人网（原校内网）最鼎盛的时候，它在社交平台的市场和用户占有率都跟QQ空间不在一个档次。虽然当时的偷菜、移车位等游戏非常火爆，但是QQ空间的迅速跟进，立即就让用户进行了转移。直到现在，很多人都会问一个问题：“为什么中国没有出现Facebook？”其实，当时QQ依靠QQ空间对人人网和开心网的阻击，彻底粉碎了中国Facebook的梦。QQ空间的迅速发展，不仅仅是为QQ从IM过渡到了一个整体的社交平台，更为其之后的Feeds广告打下了基础——如今在很多企业的眼里，QQ空间的Feeds广告都是最优质的资源。

下一个影响世界的创新会是什么？

创业初期时，马化腾完全顾不及什么是领导力，让公司活下去才是最重要的。他说：“我父母都没有想到，我这个书呆子可以开公司。所以第一步就是找合伙人，他们可以弥补我的缺陷。”

他找到的合伙人许晨晔、张志东和陈一丹都是他的中学或大学同学，曾李青则是过去的同事。这几个人各有所长，互补性强。马化腾要做的是，“用好每个人的特长，平衡各方意见”。他不是霸道总裁，管理上也不是一言堂。创业早期，腾讯几个合伙人一人一份鸡煲饭，一坐就是两三个小时，一堆公事也摆上台面，很多公司的重要战略决策起源于此。吃鸡煲饭是腾讯合伙人文化的一个象征。甚至在几个合伙人逐步退出一线管理之后，他们仍保持着良好的互动关系，没有违和声音或事件传出。陈一丹对此的解释是，几个合伙人家庭背景相似，导致大家性格相近，比较温和细致，能够接受协商制，而不是追求个人英雄主义。

然而互联网瞬息万变，腾讯这座帝国如何保持创新？这是马化腾必须面对的。

2010年，所有人都在争夺移动互联网船票，那是非生即死之战。百度、360等公司被认为在这波浪潮中没有拿出真正有影响力的产品而有掉队风险。腾讯的处境也不乐观，微博在觊觎社交网络，从PC到移动的转型中，QQ的历史包袱很沉重。马化腾坦承，这是他们遭遇的最大危机。

当时腾讯内部有三个团队参与颠覆型的产品研发，谁最先解决手机移动终端问题，谁就胜出。最后QQ邮箱团队开发出一个通过手机快速收发邮件的客户端产品，快到让用户以为不是邮件，这个产品就是后来的微信。它的研发者张小龙因此成为微信之父。

在腾讯，他们早已习惯竞争对象可能就是自己人。马化腾毫不避讳这点，甚至他觉得内部良性竞争很有必要。“自己打自己才会努力，公司才不会丢失一些大的战略机会。”

2013年，马化腾在接受央视对话采访时称，他们拿到了一张移动互联网的站票。2016年6月，他说，还没等我们坐下来船已经到岸了，要上新大陆了。因为以人工智能为代表的新一波技术浪潮才是未来，包括腾讯在内的互联网巨头都在加紧布局。AlphaGo人机大战时，马化腾和团队都很兴奋，这个沉寂多年的技术焕发新机，他们蠢蠢欲动地想做点什么。

收纳了350万个应用、日分发达2亿的应用宝7.0版本将新增一个基于AI（人工智能）和云端的机器人功能，未来用户不下载滴滴也可以在应用宝里叫车。腾讯会基于AI做更多技术层面的研发，开放给更多合作伙伴。

即便如此，马化腾仍然不知道下一个影响世界的创新会是什么。“每一次大的变革都伴随着终端的变化，智能手机兴起，一切的生态都不一样。未来随着VR（虚拟现实）、AR（增强现实）等终端越来越普及，也会发生新的应用场景变化。”

从上学开始，马化腾就钟情天文，虽然这与他创业没有直接的关系，但是对他思考问题的方式有一定的影响。他说：“喜欢天文会觉得自己很渺小，可能我们在宇宙中从来就是一个偶然。所以遇到什么事情都觉得没有什么大不了的，会让你想得更开。”

艺术家张小龙和微信

在今天，中国人对微信的依赖程度几乎达到极致。这也是腾讯帝国在新世纪第二个十年最卓越的成就。

马化腾回忆，当时有三个内部团队做微信产品，原来QQ有另外一个事业群，有新的机会做手机上的IM让他们做理所当然。另外移动QQ也在做。所以原先先天的结构不合理，后来迅速做了调整把产品聚拢。各类产品，包括新闻、游戏原来在PC和移动都是分开的，后来聚拢到一块。

“另外一个就是在广州的QQ邮箱的团队，很早接触移动办公。当时我们就想能不能在QQ邮箱开发一个APP，让每一个员工都能很方便地用手机邮件。当时就让这个团队研发手机邮箱，最后微信的机会一出来，就是这个团队五六个人把手机端的邮件系统改成微信。所以微信其实是一个邮件系统，只是快速的短邮件，后端的服务器就是原先邮箱的团队。这个团队用了一个多月就出了一个原型，张小龙带领这个团队，也有很强的产品能力。”

“微信刚出来的时候数据不好，起不来，真正的启动的因素一是语音，国外同类产品没有这个功能，有这个功能之后迅速火爆；第二是跟手机通讯录的整合，把通讯录互相匹配，最开始的启动是把QQ的关系链推过去让它生存，但是把手机通讯录导过去会导入很多高端用户，增加黏性。”

作为至关重要的人物，张小龙看上去皮肤黝黑，是一位爱打高尔夫球的中年男子，也有很多人评价，他在多数时候“扮演着一名艺术家的角色”，“他将产品视为自己所创作的艺术品”。张小龙也在这17年间，持续地进行着自我迭代与升级。多年前被以1200万元人民币卖掉的Foxmail与其说是他产品上的成功，不如说是商业上的失败——相比这点金钱，更值得惋惜的是他错过的巨大商业机会。这就是张小龙1.0，关键词是产品和技术。在微信初期，他将工具上升为平台，将服务用户的简单需求变成引导他们的喜怒哀乐，完成了第二次升级。

1998年的秋天，周鸿祎经人引荐第一次在广州见到了张小龙。他看到这名在业界已是小有名气的程序员正和十几个人挤在一间小破办公室内，周遭烟雾缭绕。看到周鸿祎之后，张小龙掐灭了手上的烟，面无表情地向他走来。张小龙所开发的Foxmail已经拥有了200万用户，是国内用户量最大的共享软件。而当年周鸿祎还仅是方正软件研发中心的一名副主任。

周鸿祎说，当年Foxmail是没有商业模式的，他经常批驳张小龙这一点，说要加广告，要赢利。张小龙说为什么非要这样？只要有用户，有情怀就好了。每一次争论，都是张小龙以长时间的沉默来结束。“这样的一个人怎么就做出了微信呢？”周鸿祎很疑惑。

Foxmail如日中天时，腾讯不过十万用户，多数人认为邮箱是比社交更大的一块领域。而正当马化腾、张朝阳欣喜地寻找风投向商业进军时，张小龙经常独自一人在深夜看用户来信，他手不离开键盘，一直按着下箭头，看着一封封信从眼前流过，每封信的停留时间不超过一秒。在张小龙眼里，Foxmail已经变成了一个大包袱，每天都有无数的人催促他往前跑，而庞大的知名度和用户量，并没有给他带来任何经济上或社会地位上的好处。

一年后，张小龙选择将Foxmail出售给了一家并不知名的互联网公司博大。消息宣布后的夜晚，他写下了一封充满伤感情绪的信，他在信中将Foxmail比喻为他精心雕塑的艺术品。“从灵魂到外表，我能数出它每一个细节，每一个典故。在我的心中，它是有灵魂的，因为它的每一段代码，都有我那一刻塑造它时的意识。我突然有了一种想反悔的冲动。”

艺术家张小龙一直是孤独的创作者，过去他走得很顺，直到这条宽阔的赛道中出现了障碍物——商业和赢利。傲游、千千静听、超级兔子等无数共享软件都被撞飞了，张小龙则侥幸进入了另一条跑道。当年他刚过31岁，但很多人认为他的个人传奇似乎就此终结。

那年夏天，百度在纳斯达克上市，所有人都以为自己眼花了——百度股价从发行价27美元飙升至122.54美元，当天暴涨354%，人们看到了资本和商业的力量。张小龙则带着博大给他的收购款，买了辆车，去了一直想去的西藏。

“怎么说呢，这个人，太单纯。”周鸿祎说。这名在商界以狡黠善战而著称的企业家，这样评价比他还大一岁的张小龙。

错过了互联网冲击纳斯达克的第一波高潮后，博大走向没落。2005年，张小龙和Foxmail被打包出售给了腾讯。张小龙在腾讯接手了QQ邮箱，并带领着QQ邮箱超越网易邮箱成为中国最大的邮件服务商，但这只是他再一次证明了自己的产品能力而已。

在很多时代，有力量的都是商人，多数艺术家都无法摆脱被商人供养而无法自主的命运。Foxmail给张小龙带来的是巨大的声望，以及颠沛流离的生活。张小龙身边一直围绕着商人，他和商人做朋友，甚至想去微软学习如何进行商业运作，但最终没有在商业上迈出一步。最后，他身边的大多兼具产品与商业天分的朋友都成功了，雷军、周鸿祎、马化腾，甚至当年采访他的记者李学凌。

有人评价，张小龙始终是一个赶潮的人，但他不在潮中。从一名程序员到一名产品经理，他学会了掌控自己的产品，但他始终无法掌控用户。然而慷慨的命运给了他第三次机会，而这次成功来得太大、太快了。

曾鸣是微信13名创始团队成员之一，他说当时包括张小龙在内的所有人都不知道要把微信做成什么样，更何况这些成员中还有一半是毫无经验的实习生。他们最初的目标是又快又稳定——这和张小龙当年做Foxmail的思路如出一辙，是一种单纯的做工具的思路。如果张小龙的产品观只是停留于此，那么他做出来的充其量只是一款还不错的聊天工具。

还有同事将张小龙比喻为一名想拍出完美大片的导演，他不是不能接受广告的植入，而是不能容忍生硬的植入，因为生硬会破坏完美。吴毅曾是财付通的助理总经理，他描述，三年前第一次见张小龙，张就在思考如何用支付联系微信和商业。“他并不排斥完美的合作，比如QQ音乐、QQ邮箱、支付。”

微信早期，张小龙负责产品，而如何接入第三方商户，如何拓展线上到线下等商业化规则，由腾讯电商副总裁戴志康负责，就连支付也是交予财付通团队来做。2012年底，Pingwest创始人骆轶航撰文说，微信商业化过慢的症结在于张与戴之间的内部分歧。

在此之后发生的戴志康离职，微信支付从财付通剥离并入微信，以及微信事业群的独立等一系列事件，你或许可以看作张小龙已有了选择——既然微信商业化不可避免，那就由微信团队自己来主导商业化。这同时也意味着以马化腾、刘炽平为代表的腾讯高层作出了选择，他们选择将商业化交给张小龙，并赋予他全权。

对内把握商业化的控制权。对外，他试图建立一整套新的体系来处理好艺术和商业的关系。举例说，腾讯内部曾有120个项目在排队接入微信，而微信的要求是先跑一个半月的数据，然后按照数据筛选。

“微信把开通什么功能，接入什么合作对象这些商业行为纳入到了产品的一部分，而对于大多数人来说，产品是商业的一部分。”一位腾讯内部高层人士说，你可以将之理解为商业化的价值观，以及艺术家的方法论。

即便到了今天，微信的商业策略也被认为是相对保守的。一名业内人士评价，张小龙对待商业化正在经历一个从逃避到试探到主导再到适应的过程，他从不把话说满，做不到的他肯定不说，做得到的他也不见得会说。

微信的商业化承载了整个腾讯转型的大理想。从目前来看，它被分为了三大步——增值服务、电商和O2O。现在它只完成了第一步，而公众号则可以让微信同时实现后两步。曾鸣说，未来微信会开放更多的入口，也会提供所有商家所期待的流量入口。

评论家们曾经以为微信只是导流的工具，而现在微信借助公众号，将腾讯强大的线上营销能力和线下商业进行连接，构建了一个庞大的线上+线下生态，在这个生态中将诞生电商、O2O、健康等各种小生态。微信和QQ的差别从某种程度上来说正如实体经济对阵虚拟经济，而后者只是前者的7%不到。

过去张小龙习惯站在商人后面，而现在他到了第一线，走上了马化腾走过的那条路——同时做产品和商业的引领者。但商业的利益重大而复杂，所以在很长一段时间内，可以想象，张小龙还会选择继续沉默。

马化腾回忆，最开始微信推出的时候，运营商很紧张了，没人发短信，电话也少了。“我要限制你，全世界有很多国家会出很多招去限制你。其实这个是势不可挡，我一直跟他们说你们放心，你们绝对会受益的，你们的语音业务下降了，但是你的流量上去了，怎么会吃亏呢？增长很难说，直到去年，数据增长比语音快，现在放心了，跟我是鱼和水的关系。”

“传祺”，传奇！

进军美国之心和一辆叫GS8的车

第一辆传祺车在七年前从广州的工厂下线。当时，新世纪进入第二个十年，私家车的市场在中国正变得越来越大。

如今，这个在中国销量第六的汽车品牌在2017年的底特律车展上成为该车展历史上首个进入主展馆的中国品牌。观察家认为，它进入美国市场的主要挑战，是与测试和满足全球最高安全及排放标准相关的高成本。“美国有着比中国严格太多的规则。”

广汽集团的业绩正在变得越来越漂亮：2016年，连续第四年入围《财富》世界500强，位居第303名，比上一年排名上升了59位。

在全球的范围内，自主创新能力已经成为区域竞争力的突出体现。今天，广东的高新技术企业数量跃居全国首位，新旧动能转换取得成效。汽车自主品牌广汽传祺的成功，就是广东汽车工业成绩单上最闪耀的一页。

广汽集团从2005年开始谋划自主品牌，到目前累计投资130亿元，建成了国内一流的研发中心和世界级的整车及发动机工厂，推出了广汽传祺自主品牌。在J.D.Power发布的

2015中国新车质量研究报告（IQS）中，广汽传祺连续三年蝉联中国品牌品质冠军，排名第八，与广汽丰田齐名。在销量上，广汽传祺从2011年进入市场，销量呈跨越式增长，2011年1.7万辆，2014年11.6万辆。2015年中国汽车市场同比增长仅4.7%，广汽传祺的销量达19万辆，同比增长63%，全年实现销售收入177亿元，而传祺首款SUV——GS4的月销量跻身全国SUV前三名。据了解，在广汽集团启动实施的“十三五”战略规划中，提出了“1513”战略，其中“1”个重点就是举全集团之力发展自主品牌，实现自主品牌事业的跨越式发展。

2016年，广汽传祺取得销量和品牌的“双突破”。2017年1月，广汽传祺延续上一年良好势头，继续保持增长态势。1月份，广汽传祺累计销售46273辆，同比增长60%，增幅位居国内汽车主机厂之首，刷新中国本土品牌新高度。其中，上市仅三个月的“旗舰级豪华大7座SUV”——传祺GS8，1月份共售出9418辆，连续三个月大幅增长。

传祺GS8单月销量9418辆，与丰田汉兰达、福特锐界并肩，形成三强鼎立的中大型SUV市场格局。这是中国本土品牌第一次在与合资对手直面对决当中，表现出坚挺的姿态。传祺GS8在16万～25万元这一中国本土品牌从未染指的价格区间成功立足，这在中国汽车历史上，同样是第一次。

按照如此高的发展速度，传祺GS8有望超越汉兰达和锐界，在细分市场中冲击第一。现在看GS8的销售势头，也是奔着这个“小目标”去的。一旦实现，无疑是可以载入中国汽车史册的事件，让所有为中国汽车崛起而奋斗三十余年的汽车人为之振奋，也为后来者坚定信心。

不仅如此，传祺GS8的热销，让广汽传祺彻底摆脱“一条腿”走路的尴尬。热销车型从一款增至两款，产品结构趋于合理，车型售价区间进一步扩大。并助推广汽传祺在广汽集团总销量比重从22.38%提升至27.55%，提高5个百分点，逼近30%大关。

以GS8热销为标志，广汽传祺正在引领广东汽车业从“广东制造”迈向“广东创造”，将“中国制造”的影响力从产品跃升至品牌。在不远的将来，随着广汽传祺海外战略的逐步推进，尤其是2019年正式登陆美国市场，还将助推“中国品牌”影响力从中国市场扩大到全球市场。“广汽传祺将成为中国汽车领军品牌，年产销100万辆会比最初预计的2020年提前实现。”在2017年北美底特律车展前夜，广汽集团执行委员会副主任、广汽乘用车公司总经理郁俊信心满满地直言。

传祺GS8的出现绝非偶然，没有任何侥幸的成分，这来源于广汽传祺坚持高端的发展战略，坚持正向开发，坚持国际标准。从刚开始的GA5，再到GS5、GS4，传祺一直是平均单车价格最高的本土汽车品牌，平均单车售价甚至高于一些合资品牌。传祺GS8到来之前，广汽传祺GS4平均单车售价约为14万元。GS8到来之后，广汽传祺将平均单车售价一举提升到接近20万元的崭新高度，为后续车型赢得宽阔的战略空间。

自亮相以来，传祺GS8“超硬朗霸气外观”的造型设计，获得媒体与消费者一致好评。然而，出色的外观设计，仅是GS8取得如此出色成绩的一方面原因。传祺GS8还提供“全地形无畏驾控”“大格局七座空间”“新视野智能互联”，以及全面超越同级的品质与性价比优势，全面领先用户期待。

上市以来，传祺GS8接连斩获“年度中国品牌SUV”“年度最具实力大型SUV”“2016十大强烈推荐新车奖”“年度人气SUV”等国内外近百项大奖，受到权威媒体和业界的广泛赞誉，实现了销量和口碑双丰收。

与此同时，在J.D.Power中国新车质量研究报告中，传祺品牌已经连续四年蝉联中国品牌第一，品质超越了绝大部分合资产品，消费者的普遍信赖成为传祺产品热销的内在因素。

在消费升级市场趋势中，品牌力和车型品质在汽车企业竞争中发挥的作用日益关键。传祺GS8全面搭载广汽传祺在研发、设计、制造等领域的创新成果。

在中国市场，只要打开20万～25万元这一价位的市场，就获得全价格区间的市场通行证。丰田、本田都是在凯美瑞和雅阁热销而确定其全球主流汽车主机厂的江湖地位。传祺GS8的成功之于广汽传祺，也是具有里程碑式的意义。传祺GS8之后，广汽传祺上可以进入豪华车市场，与讴歌、英菲尼迪、凯迪拉克竞争，往下可以在B级、A+级、A级、A0级等各个细分市场大展拳脚。

广汽传祺不是第一个决心坚持高端的中国品牌，当然也不是最后一个。过去十年，中国汽车走一条曲曲折折的弯路，事实证明，“品牌向上”和“坚持正向研发”才是中国本土汽车品牌应该努力的方向。进入所有标准苛刻的中高端市场，在某种程度上，就是向所有消费者展示自己的能力。

GS8将中国本土汽车品牌——乃至中国制造——拔擢到新的高度。这种高度，不是来自于虚高的定价，也非口头的吹嘘，是实实在在的订单，和真真切切的销量数字。在16万～25万元这个价格区间，三个月实现4万张订单，和9418辆的月销量，不能说后无来者，但至少在此前，是没有先例的。

“中国制造”的代表，是科技界的华为，也是以格力、海尔为首的家电企业。要拼齐“中国制造”完整的版图，必须得有汽车企业。在汽车企业中实现全力冲刺并冲线，一个国家制造业的形象才能在全球范围内树立起来。世界汽车制造业在迎来英国、美国、德国、日本、韩国之后，随着以广汽传祺为首的中国汽车品牌的崛起，也将迎来中国品牌的身影。

技术创新没有捷径

沿着“传祺”生产线一路参观，仿佛置身于一个科幻的世界：机器人挥动巨大的手臂精确焊接、装配，无人驾驶推车将各种部件准确送到工位；这一端一个个空的车壳子鱼贯而入，那一端一辆辆崭新的“传祺”整车鱼贯而出……

对于“传祺”含义的解释，广汽集团董事长曾庆洪说，祺是吉祥、幸福的意思，我们要让自主品牌汽车向所有用户传递吉祥和幸福。

然而要实现这个美好的祝愿并不容易。“‘传祺’刚上马的时候，我的内心是崩溃的。”广汽集团副总经理、乘用车公司董事长吴松一直具体负责传祺系列产品的生产与销售，在广汽其他几个合资品牌广汽本田、广汽丰田等赚得盆满钵满的时候，起步阶段的“传祺”却连续数年巨额亏损。市场对自主品牌汽车质量与性能的天生不信任，他还只是窝火；集团内部兄弟单位的冷嘲热讽就让他哭笑不得了——你们谁不好好干，发配你们去“传祺”。

面对合资品牌一统市场的巨大压力，自主品牌汽车竟真的不能在全球最大且高速发展的国内市场上赢得一席之地？

对此他们主动调低“传祺”产销任务，但不惜一切狠抓产品质量。曾庆洪说，“传祺”品牌是靠品质打出来的，没有“品”就没有“牌”，“传祺”首要的是不惜一切抓产品品质，他就不相信“传祺”品牌打不出来。

经过多年刻苦努力，走过了自主品牌汽车最艰难的市场启动期，广汽传祺开始以优异的品质和高性价比逐步走进千家万户。2016年1—10月，广汽传祺全系销量29.6万辆，同比增长126%，发展速度和赢利水平位居中国汽车品牌前列。

在广汽自主品牌汽车刚上马的时候，无论是业内还是普通消费者几乎没人看好，因为“传祺”当时没有人才、没有资金、没有技术，有人开玩笑说这是一个“三无”公司。最关键的问题是，广汽没有整车设计与研发能力。连整车都不能设计，谈什么自主品牌?

但谁也没有料到，广汽能投入100多亿元建成国际先进的汽车研究院，从2006年成立时仅有三四十名研发人员，到今天已建立起一支三千余人的研发人才队伍。目前这里拥有整车、动力总成、新能源等十余个先进实验室和含焊接、涂装、总装、机加工在内的试制工厂，以及汽车调校专用试验跑道，具备整车整机及关键部件研发、试制、试验能力。这些都为广汽传祺提供了源源不断的发展力。“广汽研究院一年可以推出五个新车型。”广汽研究院副院长张帆介绍说。

从没有整车开发能力到新车型推出一批，研发一批，储备一批，广汽研究院已经向市场推出一系列车型，实现产品全覆盖。“广汽研究院的成功和自主品牌整车设计能力的提升说明，技术创新没有捷径，必须一步一个脚印。”曾庆洪说。

“自主品牌汽车不会一帆风顺，但我始终相信未来中国汽车市场一定是自主品牌汽车主导，中国自主品牌汽车也一定能走向世界。”作为我国汽车工业崛起全过程的见证者和参与者，曾庆洪表示，不仅是普通的乘用车和商用车，新能源汽车领域更是充满前景。

新能源汽车一直都被寄予厚望，然而这个研发过程也是相当曲折。“一大笔钱投下去，没有什么明显起色，甚至只能证实此路不通，心里的滋味相当复杂。”曾庆洪表示。但他相信，新能源汽车一定能像现在的普通汽车一样走进千家万户。

“研发外脑”马可的故事

Marco Mario Gilardi（马可·马里奥·吉拉尔迪）的办公室位于番禺化龙镇广汽研究院内。作为广汽研究院首席专业总师，马可全程参与了广汽集团首款自主品牌轿车“传祺”的研发工作，发挥重要作用。广东省汽车工程学会理事长、广汽研究院原院长黄向东形容马可在传祺开发中的重要性就像桌子的一条腿：“一张桌子有四条腿，缺失了一条，那就麻烦了，站不住。”

像马可这样的“外脑”在广东还有很多，近年来，外国专家的引进成为广东人才引进的“重头戏”。广东省统计局发布的数据显示，2014、2015年广东聘请境外来中国大陆工作专家分别为13.21万人次和12.99万人次，分别占全国比重为21.3%和20.8%，聘请境外专家人数居全国第一位。这些外国专家用自己的热情和专业为广东的创新驱动发展贡献力量。

“十一五”之初，广州提出要生产自主品牌的汽车。2006年7月，广汽集团以原广州汽车技术中心为基础，成立了广汽研究院，专门负责广州自主品牌汽车的研发。原华南理工大学教授、广汽集团副总经理黄向东出任首任院长。

刚成立的广汽研究院，除了三个服务部门，仅有四个技术部门，研发人员三十余人，而且多数是经验欠缺的年轻人，要自主研发出自己的汽车十分不易，招揽人才成为首要任务。就在这个时候，黄向东在意大利都灵遇到了25年未见的老朋友马可。

"在广汽和菲亚特的一个合作项目中我见到了一些从广东来的人，仔细一看，居然是黄向东！"谈起两个人的再次相遇，马可说这是一种缘分。

20世纪80年代，黄向东曾在菲亚特研究中心工作，那时马可刚刚毕业进入菲亚特，二人就在同一间办公室。再相遇时，马可已在菲亚特工作了近30年，而黄向东回国后也一直深耕汽车行业，先后在华南理工大学担任教授、在广汽集团担任副总经理，然后又被授命组建广汽研究院。

当时，菲亚特有业务在中国，马可常常到中国出差，对中国的印象很好。黄向东向他讲述研发自主品牌汽车的想法，他就常常过来"友情客串"，对年轻的研究人员给予一些技术上的指点。

"当时的广汽研究院非常小，场地也没有，只在华南理工大学租了一层楼，马可完全是出于帮助老同事、老朋友，常常过来'客串指导'。"当年在意大利工作时，黄向东就对马可的人品非常赞赏。

2007年12月和2008年4月，经过多番艰苦谈判和细节磋商，广汽集团先后与菲亚特有关方面签订了发动机和底盘平台技术转让合同。马可被调到该公司负责对口广汽的业务。这个时候，广州打造自主品牌汽车的思路已相当明确，并进入实质性准备阶段，对人才的渴求更甚。黄向东想到直接将马可"挖"到广汽。

"你愿意来广汽工作吗？"黄向东问马可。马可用他一贯的幽默作答：“为什么我们合作这么久你才问这个问题？”

离开工作29年的菲亚特，将妻子独自留在意大利，马可说“在这里找到了激情和目标”。面对黄向东抛过来的橄榄枝，马可虽然有意，但仍有犹豫。马可在菲亚特已经工作了近30年，职位不低，本可安安稳稳做到退休。而且当时两个女儿已长大成人，出国发展，如果他再离开，妻子将孤身一人留在意大利。对他来说，离乡背井来中国并非易事。

菲亚特也对其进行了挽留。“有人跟我说，菲亚特当时已经引进了克莱斯勒公司，如果你想有一些海外工作经验，也可以去克莱斯勒公司。”而且，与克莱斯勒公司相比，当时的广汽在国际上只是个名不见经传的小公司。

不过，马可最终还是选择了广汽。很多人不理解他的选择。但他自己形容为“听从内心的选择”。“我突然发现，我这29年都在菲亚特度过，我不想再继续了。”马可觉得，自己需要有一个新的挑战、新的转折，“如果在菲亚特按部就班，我觉得也是不错的，但我总觉得如果自己足够好的话，来到中国也能干出一番新天地。”

“在之前的合作中，我对广汽产生了好感，因为在这里我找到了激情和目标。”讲述起当年的选择时，马可说他是被广汽的氛围和广汽员工的激情所感染。“在和广汽员工接触之后，我越来越觉得这里的年轻人很有激情去把这个事情做好。这里的领导也有决心去做一个最大最强的汽车行业领军企业。所以我对这里的人和事，越来越有好感和兴趣。”过去的积累也给了马可很好的储备，“我希望有一个从零开始的机会，翻开新的篇章，但也可以说不是从零开始，因为我以前也有了很好的积累。”

一开始什么都没有，连底盘都没有，研发出首款自主品牌，马可的重要性就像一张桌子不可或缺的那一条腿。2009年11月，马可加盟广汽。这时的广汽条件仍然简陋，甚至连实验室都没建起来。而当时广州的目标是：要在2010年广州举办的亚运会上，让来宾坐上广汽自主品牌汽车。广州市相关领导将其作为“广州市自主创新一号工程”。

一开始，很多人觉得这是一个“不可能的任务”。马可上任后，开始带领年轻的团队向目标进发。他主要负责整车集成和车辆底盘两个环节的研发。为了顺利完成任务，马可周末几乎都不休息，还要到外地做实验。“在襄阳，我们做整车实验，在包头做沙地实验，在黑龙江做冰雪实验。”

当然，他的团队都是这样的节奏。“其实周末加班的并不只是我自己，我们有很多人都这样。我工作，他们也工作，不是我推着他们，而是他们推着我。”两年内研发出首款自主品牌汽车，困难当然不小。用黄向东的话说，一开始什么都没有，连底盘都没有。但是，这个团队克服了重重困难。2010年9月，广州亚运会前夕，广汽集团首款自主品牌轿车“传祺”终于下线，实现了广州人多年的汽车“自主梦”。

按计划，500辆传祺轿车作为第16届亚运会官方指定用车，为来自亚洲及世界各地的贵宾提供服务。“这整个过程中，都有马可的身影。”黄向东说。

“我的团队刚开始很弱，都没有经验，就需要有人带。这个关键时候，需要顶梁柱。马可就是顶梁柱之一。”黄向东说，当队伍慢慢成长起来后，他的顶梁柱的作用仍然存在。“这个团队要行，这个团队的核心团队就必须行，马可就是核心团队中最出色的成员之一。”2014年9月，中国政府授予马可外国人士最高荣誉奖项的——国家“友谊奖”；2015年4月，马可成功入选国家第四批“外专千人计划”。不过，马可并不认为自己是“导师”的角色。“我从来不教他们什么东西，我只是和他们一起工作。”他说。

广东引进外国专家已成常态。省外国专家局提供的数据显示，五年来，每年来粤工作的境外专家超过13万人次，占全国1/5，居于首位；累计引进海外人才3.7万人，其中诺贝尔奖获得者、发达国家院士、终身教授等129人，入选中央“外专千人计划”19人。如何才能用好这些“外脑”，让他们为广东的创新驱动更好地服务？黄向东认为，首先是外在氛围，要有吸引人的优惠条件。他认为，无论是广东省还是广州市，现在都不缺优惠条件了。

“但也有很多企业，人才来了也发挥不好，很多时候就是因为不被信任。”曾引进多位外国专家的黄向东说，要用好“外脑”，真正的人才来了之后要能够被信任，要有委以重任的平台，使其长期、稳定地发挥作用。“现在很多企业，引进的人才总是干不了多久就走了，什么原因？那一定是企业在文化、在信任上出了问题。别人干得不开心啊，或者在这里干不了什么实事。”

“另外，比如说，高层次的专家通常和我们一般员工不是一个薪酬体系。如果他来了以后，员工都不喜欢他，觉得他拿那么多钱还不如我，这也是个问题。”黄向东认为，优化配置是一门艺术，也一门技术，“关键是这个企业的主要领导如何看待人才，如何真心真意用人才、爱人才。”

“人才有优点，有缺点。他一方面很强，一方面很弱。要容忍他弱的一面，发挥他特长的一面。不能想着利用利用人家，不当作自己人，这样肯定发挥不了人才的作用。”黄向东说。

广东“无人机”翱翔全球天空

进入迪拜的亿航传奇

这个消息迅速攀登上很多主流媒体的头版，被很多人称为“广东的骄傲”。迪拜当地媒体Arabian Business2月13日援引迪拜交通局的声明报道称，“亿航184”在乘客座位前面配有触摸屏，乘客在地图上选择目的地后，无人机将按预设航路飞抵目的地。飞行实际上受地面控制中心监测和控制。迪拜民航局已经颁发了试飞许可，阿联酋电信负责提供无人机和地面控制中心之间通信的4G数据网络。

英国媒体BBC（英国广播公司）在14日报道此事时，援引英国西英格兰大学航空专家怀特（Steve Wright）博士的观点称：真实载人飞行前，飞机要进行1000小时以上的无人飞行测试。

广东的无人机，正在呈现着“翱翔全球天空”的光荣和梦想。继大疆一骑绝尘地占领全球消费级无人机市场之后，行业应用的技术也在出海。除了亿航的载人飞行器，同样位于广州的极飞科技率先在日本设立分公司，投入日本的农业植保领域中。撇开无人机玩具，无人机的海外走俏可以说是产业级取胜，是高附加值的制造业的一次输出。

2016年1月在美国，“亿航184”在国际消费类电子产品展览会上首秀，号称全球首款低空中短途自动驾驶载人飞行器。“184”意指1名乘客、8个螺旋桨、4支外伸机臂。亿航公司官网介绍称，净重240千克的“亿航184”使用纯电动力，海平面续航时间可达25分钟，平均巡航速度60千米/小时，最高设计飞行高度是海拔3500米。该无人机额定载重100千克，后备箱容量为可放入1个18吋行李箱。此外，“亿航184”还设有独立密匙为通信系统进行数据加密。

公开资料显示，广州亿航由胡华智、熊逸放创始于2014年。当年12月获得由GGV纪源资本领投的1000万美元A轮融资，又在2015年8月获得4200万美元的B轮融资。目前公司团队约300人。

一个航模迷、技术控，一个曾留学海外，还有一个擅长营销，2014年，三个创业者在广州相遇，一家名叫亿航的无人机公司在天河诞生。从此，这家代表着广州的无人机公司异军突起蓬勃发展。

2014年，从美国杜克大学毕业回国创业的熊逸放，在北京遇到了正在向投资人展示无人机的胡华智。当年正是无人机风生水起的一年，位于深圳的无人机领军企业大疆，在全球商用无人机市场中占有近70%的市场份额，而越来越多的厂商开始进入无人机领域，小米、腾讯等互联网企业更是多次传出跨界做无人机的消息。而彼时的广州，正是无人机发展的空白地。

当熊逸放又认识了销售人才杨镇全后，三人一拍即合，2014年，他们在广州开始了亿航的创业之路。他们瞄准“傻瓜式”无人机操作市场开发产品，在手机上安装一个APP即可轻松地操控无人机飞行，还可以让无人机自动跟随用户。

站在无人机产业风口上的亿航，像火箭一样快速蹿升，成立仅半年多就融资1000万美元，估值在6个月之内翻了25倍，还被美国杂志《快公司》评为2014中国年度最创新公司50强，位列第二。杨镇全说，广州是国际化的贸易大都会，而且政策和供应链等都非常符合做硬件的环境，他们非常感谢这片创新创业热土，给了亿航“飞一般”的成长速度。

2017年的元宵节，广州在海心沙创造了一项浪漫的吉尼斯纪录——1000架无人机编队花式表演，似漫天飞舞的流星，直升百米夜空。它们“画”出金鸡报晓、喜迎新年、祖国河山等光影佳作，当场创造了“数量最多的无人机编队飞行表演”吉尼斯世界纪录。这场“千机变”表演，就是来自亿航的“广州智造”。

元宵节当晚，当时钟指向9时。“起飞”，对讲机中倒计时声音刚落，广州交响乐团的60位艺术家们的指间流淌出著名交响乐《黄河·第三乐章》，1000架型号为GHOSTDRONE2.0的智能航拍机伴随着音乐冉冉升起。与海心沙隔江相望的花城广场上人头攒动，观众齐齐仰头观看目不转睛，一幕幕“天幕流星”花式映月，带来了最梦幻的体验。在这场表演背后，亿航在两年前就开始研发无人机编队表演技术，决定采用编队无人机实时通信网络，确保即使单个无人机出现故障或受到通信干扰时，都不会影响整体任务的完成。

本次破吉尼斯纪录的最大亮点，是后台只需一个人、一台电脑、一键控制。技术人员说，2016年央视春节联欢晚会中广州分会场进行的无人机编队表演，其实是从全国各地邀请了许多顶尖飞手，用遥控器控制其飞行，降低技术难度和风险。如今表演阵队达到了1000架，地面也不可能让1000名飞手实地操控。因此，工程师们设计出一套智能高效的无人机编队远程操控系统，会同一时间告诉每一架飞机该怎么飞、位置在哪儿、队列如何切换、灯光颜色如何变化等。

2017年，全世界的“朋友圈”都被各种无人机编队飞行表演刷屏。2017年央视春晚，无人机身影再次出现，一款口袋无人机在《满城烟花》节目中，完成了高难度的室内舞台大型编队飞行，成为整个春晚科技流的颜值和实力担当。国际科技公司都将无人机视为利器，大举进军文化娱乐产业，树立良好的品牌形象。

从2016年央视春节联欢晚会中广州分会场一炮而红，到2016年夏季达沃斯论坛开幕前夕，36架无人机在世界经济论坛创始人兼主席克劳斯·施瓦布一行前翩翩起舞，到如今的创吉尼斯世界纪录，都说明了广州以科技元素打造“智造”城市的渴望。中国作为无人机产业发展最为如火如荼的市场，广州也成为目前最为耀眼的无人机舞台。

对天空极度痴迷的汪滔

除了广州亿航，广东还有一位无人机巨头——深圳大疆。大疆无人机的产品占据了全球民用小型无人机约70%的市场份额，其销售市场主要集中在欧美国家，占其过去总销售额的80%。全球无人机行业第一位亿万富翁是一位叫汪滔的中国人。这是《福布斯》杂志下的定义，汪滔就是大疆的老板。

大疆现在一年可以售出了几十万架无人机——许多是其主力机型“大疆精灵”（Phantom）系列。在2009年至2014年间，大疆的销售额以每年两到三倍的速度增长。2015年5月，大疆从Accel Partners那里获得了7500万美元投资，而持有公司约45%股份的汪滔的个人资产将达到接近40亿美元。

全球的目光都在关注这家公司。无人机在大规模用于商用：在金球奖颁奖典礼上，无人机实时传送航拍画面；在尼泊尔7.8级大地震中，救援人员依靠无人机来绘制受灾地区的地图；美国爱荷华州的农场主还利用无人机监测麦田；Facebook将利用自有无人机产品向非洲农场地区提供无线互联网接入；大疆的无人机还出现在《权力的游戏》和最新一部《星球大战》电影的拍摄现场。

汪滔的办公室门上写着两行汉字——“只带脑子”和“不带情绪”。这位大疆的掌门人遵守着这些规则，他是一位言辞激烈却相当理性的领导人，每周工作80多个小时，办公桌旁边放着一张单人床。

汪滔出生于1980年，他对天空的痴迷始于小学，在读了一本讲述红色直升机探险故事的漫画书之后，他开始对天空充满了想象。在汪滔16岁的时候，他在一次考试中得了高分，父母为此奖励了他一架梦寐以求的遥控直升机。然而，他不久便将这个复杂的东西弄坏了，几个月后才收到从香港发来的用于更换的零部件。

由于成绩不是那么的出类拔萃，汪滔考取美国一流大学的梦想也破灭了。当时，汪滔最想上的大学是麻省理工学院和斯坦福大学，但在申请遭到拒绝后，他只好退而求其次，选择了香港科技大学，在那里学习电子工程专业。在上大学的头三年，汪滔一直没找到自己的人生目标，但在大四的时候他开发了一套直升机飞行控制系统，他的人生由此改变。

为了这最后一个小组项目，汪滔可谓付出了一切，甚至不惜逃课，还熬夜到凌晨5点。虽然他开发的这个机载计算机的悬停功能在班级展示前一晚出了问题，但他付出的心血并没有白费。香港科技大学机器人技术教授李泽湘（Li Zexiang）慧眼识珠，发现了汪滔的领导才能以及对技术的理解能力。

于是，在他的引荐下，这个性格倔强的学生读上了研究生。“汪滔是否比别人更聪明，这我倒是不清楚。”李泽湘说，“但是，学习成绩优异的人不见得在工作中就表现得非常突出。”李泽湘是大疆的早期顾问及投资者，现在则是该公司董事会主席，持有

10%的股份。

汪滔最初在大学宿舍中制造飞行控制器的原型，2006年他和自己的两位同学来到了中国制造业中心——深圳。他们在一套三居室的公寓中办公，汪滔将他在大学获得的奖学金的剩余部分全部拿出来搞研究。

随着核心团队的建立，汪滔继续开发产品，并开始向国外业余爱好者销售，这些人从德国和新西兰等国家给他发来电子邮件。在美国，《连线》杂志主编安德森创办了无人机爱好者的留言板DIY Drones，上面的一些用户提出无人机应该从单旋翼设计向四旋翼设计转变，因为四旋翼飞行器价格更便宜，也更容易进行编程。因此，大疆开始开发具有自动驾驶功能的更为先进的飞行控制器。开发完成以后，汪滔带着它们到一些小型贸易展上推销，比如2011年在印第安纳州曼西市举办的无线电遥控直升机大会。

到2012年晚些时候，大疆已经拥有了一款完整无人机所需要的一切元素：软件、螺旋桨、支架、平衡环以及遥控器。最终，该公司在2013年1月发布“大疆精灵”，这是第一款可以随时起飞的预装四旋翼飞行器：它在开箱一小时内就能飞行，而且第一次坠落不会造成解体。得益于简洁和易用的特性，“大疆精灵”撬动了非专业无人机市场。

据说，汪滔还需要处理形形色色的商业间谍活动问题。他断定过去两年涌现出来的一些国内无人机创业公司曾非法获取大疆的设计。

近几年，大疆在海外开疆拓土，陆续设立了17个办事处，以轻量的办事机构模式在各城市驻扎。具体来看，在日本有销售和技术支持、在韩国有销售办公室、在德国和荷兰有技术支持和物流支持、在北美好莱坞有销售和市场、在帕罗奥图有研发中心、在纽约也有办公室。

在海外乃至全球的消费级无人机市场上，大疆可谓在终端制霸。从2011年到2015年，每年的营业收入在以3到5倍的速度增长，根据大疆方面的数据，2015年达到60亿元销售额，随着基数的增大，2016年相比2015年销售额增速放缓，上涨幅度在60%～70%之间，以65%换算，大疆2016年销售额约为99亿元。

目前，大疆80%以上的营业额来自海外，北美是最大市场，其次是欧洲，2016年澳大利亚营业额增幅较大。

无人机变身辛勤劳动的农民

广州极飞电子科技有限公司是广东另一个名声赫赫的无人机品牌。在极飞看来，无人机就是一位辛勤劳动的农民。她正在进入日本植保市场，与雅马哈展开竞技。

2016年11月，雅马哈新款农业无人机Fazer R正式上市，售价为1342.44万日元（约合人民币87.11万元），配备了燃油喷射发动机，可提供20.6kW的功率输出；可在空中向着植物喷洒农药，每次能喷洒农田近4公顷，最多可携带32升药剂。同年10月，极飞也发布了该公司最新一款P20植保无人机、农业无人机飞控，并宣布推出植保无人机销售和租赁业务。据了解，全新P20 2017款植保无人机系统包括无人机、GNSS RTK定位设备（手持测绘器、移动基站、固定基站）、A2智能手持终端、药箱、灌药机、智能电池和充电器，售价为94999元，裸机每架48500元。而普通用户还可以选择租赁P20植保无人机，租金则是按照作业量算。

成立于2007年的极飞自2012年开始便研发农业植保无人机，在农业无人机领域取得了重大突破，获得多项国家及国际技术专利。2017年1月24日，极飞科技宣布成立日本子公司，正式在日本铺开P20植保无人机销售及植保服务网络。

在极飞科技创始人彭斌的眼中，极飞的农业无人机通过在国内这么多年的发展，在技术与生产制造上都拥有一定能力，甚至达到了一定的领先水平，进入日本市场是因为日本的农业跟中国面临一样的问题，那就是人口老龄化、劳动力成本急剧上升、农场人口减少等。但是这些问题在日本比中国更早到来，更需要这类自动化的农业无人机。

据英国《金融时报》报道，在日本以外很少人知道，自20世纪80年代以来无人机就开始在日本的农田扮演重要角色，那时候摩托车生产商雅马哈研发出了无人直升机，即用于喷洒农药和播种粮食。日本家庭的餐桌上，每两碗米饭中就有一碗是用雅马哈无人机灌溉出来的。

在中国无人机领域，许多公司都选择多向发展，但是极飞却选择了首先专注于农业这个相对“冷门”的领域。截至2016年10月，极飞科技旗下的极飞农业已经组建了约800人的服务团队，在全国14个省份的作业面积超过了200万亩，为近10万用户提供了无人机植保服务。并且在新疆和河南建立了极飞服务总站。

“我们其实探索过很多行业的运用，包括物流、警用、军用等，但是在探索的过程中，我们最终选择了农业。”彭斌说，农业的市场更广阔，它可以给像极飞这类创业公司更好地施展拳脚的机会；另外，农业里面有大量的空间可以用科技去改变，这也是极飞当初创业的目的，希望自己创造的产品或掌握的技能能够解决某一项技术问题。

农业分为四个基本环节，在整个农业的生产周期中，耕地、种植、管理和收割是四个基本要素，而极飞参与的是管理环节。

“极飞通过两条通道来服务农户，第一条通道是极飞有一个自营团队，可以给政府或大型农户的种植土地提供喷洒服务，只要进行每亩多少钱的结算即可，例如每一亩地10元或15元，不需要购买无人机；第二条通道，极飞有很多合作伙伴，他们可以给当地农场、种植户提供服务。”彭斌说，“随着农村土地越来越集中，土地流转越来越快，越来越多的农场需要这样的专业服务。未来农业一定是一个越来越分工细致的行业。”

广东高校
创客精英

陈第：险象环生，步步为营的公司故事

华南理工大学2006级计算机专业毕业生陈第，在大学毕业三年后进入《福布斯》中文版“中国30位30岁以下创业者排行榜”。《福布斯》中文版对上榜者这样评价：这些已表现出技术、产品和商业模式创新能力的青年人，已经具备很强的创业精神和颠覆能力。

在华南理工大学计算机科学与工程学院的师生眼中，读书时候的陈第是个“技术控”“比赛控”。“我不喜欢做书面作业，但是并不代表我不爱学习。”陈第的好学不仅表现在他热衷实践、乐于动手实验，更体现在他强烈的自学精神上。大二那年，为了跟随曾经在全国挑战杯上获奖的师兄一起开发一项游戏，陈第在完成课堂学习要求之外，几乎天天泡在图书馆，钻研更多的计算机技术知识，也几乎每一天都是最后一个离开图书馆。

“华工的学术氛围很自由、很开放，学院也鼓励我们多动手，这些为我后来的创业选择提供了很大帮助。”陈第说。也就是从大二那年开始，陈第陆续参加了“IBM主机应用创新大赛”“微软精英大挑战”“全国大学生信息安全竞赛”等大型比赛。“在学校的时候就能接触这些著名企业，做一些实训项目，对我的动手能力促进很大。”陈第很感谢母校为他提供了很多锻炼身手的机会，这些平台不仅让他学习了如何进行项目管理、团队合作，也让他尝试并确定了适合自己的发展方向，这一切都为他自己创业奠定了良好的基础。

其实，出生于潮汕的陈第，从小就有着自己创业的梦想，自从参加各种比赛并小有收获后，有种叫“天生的商业嗅觉”的东西就袭击了他的大脑，他心里开始反复比较、思量，从大型机到PC市场，经过陈第不自觉的“商业风险评估”，他决定从手机小游戏做起。

“年轻人觉得这个好玩，又是一个充满机会的新兴市场。”2007年的夏天，陈第跑去中华广场那里买来一部便宜的二手智能手机，和几个同学编写手机程序，当陈第发觉这些手机游戏可以如此“酷炫”时，他干脆拉了一帮热爱技术的同学成立了工作室，开始天天猫在实验室里捣鼓各类手机应用软件。蓝牙三国杀、蓝牙斗地主、3D桌球……这些软件被放在网络上供免费下载，很快就有了每天2000多次的下载量。但很快，陈第的团队陷入了收费与否的窘境，面对开发者与用户之间无法避免的矛盾，他说：“有些同学很享受编程的乐趣，但我更享受将技术转化为生产力。我宁愿花时间搞清楚如何做好一个产品把它商业化。”

大一的时候，陈第就做了一家类似携程网的网站，但出现了两个问题：与商户签约辛苦且效率低；流量太差导致业务很难开展。陈第读的是计算机专业，他意识到创业的第一个教训：一定要形成技术核心竞争力。

大二陈第开始研究技术创业，基本上形成了创始团队的雏形。做了IBM的大型机项目，当时还想做全国信用系统。但现在想来对于一个初创团队来讲，这个项目很难商业化。当时这个项目拿了优秀应用奖，但没有商业化。他当时还参加了一些微软的比赛，主要是基于微软的框架开发的一些游戏和应用。在奥运期间，陈第来到北京微软这里实习，学到很多，“当时我意识到PC创业的时期已经过去了。”

2008年，陈第团队参加了成都电子科技大学举办的全国大学生信息安全的大赛，提交了一个手机应用，那个应用的设计原理是记录用户输入密码时的解锁力度，即使别人知道密码但没有掌握解锁时的力度和节奏也不能打开。代码很简单量也很小，但评价相当高，还获了二等奖。“这给了我们很大信心，觉得移动互联网是可以创业的方向。”

2010年，即将毕业的陈第面临着三个选择：保送读研、去新加坡参加交换生项目、自己创业。最后一个选择似乎最不“靠谱”——辅导员希望他珍惜保研机会，团队里有人离开去了腾讯实习。“陈第，你创业我们就跟你创业，你读研我们就一起读研！”就在陈第纠结不知如何选择的时候，两位同班同学，也是他团队一直以来的核心队员李展铿和张暖晖，坚定地宣布“同盟”。巧合的是，多年之后，人们把这一年称为“移动互联网元年”。

2015年4月1日，有米五周岁。陈第在官网发布了有米移动广告平台五周年的讲话视频。他激情洋溢地说，五年前，怀着让“中国的智能手机开发者有饭吃”的朴素愿望，有米作为中国第一家移动广告平台成立了。最值得欣喜的就是，我们帮助了中国近万的广告主伙伴推广其APP或手机网页等产品，更帮助超过10万的独立开发者伙伴通过广告获得盈利，同时，累计促进全球超过10亿用户通过移动广告参与到移动互联网的信息传播中。如今，创业团队从最初的十来人发展到了360多人；从广州总部开始到北京、上海、香港等公司的设立，从中国市场走向国际市场！在接下来的几年里，互联网金融、O2O、智能硬件、医疗和教育等各个行业与移动互联网的紧密结合将成为这个小时代的突出亮点，有米将会积极参与其中，作为众多产品服务的推广者继续发挥其价值，同时帮助更多的开发者、媒体，以及新兴的内容创造者获得盈利。

他也再次强调了“有米”名称的内涵：大家有米，才是真的有米！

2015年起，有米积极布局实施全球化战略，建立专注于国际业务的全球化移动广告平台Adxmi。资料显示，Adxmi的广告业务覆盖Android与IOS双平台，广告流量遍布港澳台、东南亚（泰国、越南、印度尼西亚、菲律宾、马来西亚）、北美、南美、欧洲等区域，覆盖全球超过200个国家和地区，与全球1500家媒介渠道有战略合作关系。

米汇平台是有米除了“有米广告+Adxmi”APP广告业务外，在社会化营销板块的又一重要布局。其定位是专注于社会化媒体的营销平台。目前米汇平台已积累1000多个意见领袖，合作了超过10万个微信行业公众号，累计粉丝过亿。

至此，有米已布局移动互联网各流量入口，汇聚各方强势资源，打造移动互联网营销生态圈。从公开资料来看，有米的营收规模、净利润、APP覆盖规模、终端覆盖数量都属于行业一线水平，其看准在长尾市场的发展优势，拒绝了所有被并购，坚持独立发展，立志做中国最大的独立移动营销平台。

当年，有米获选2015年《福布斯》中国最具潜力非上市公司TOP10以及2015年中国最佳移动广告平台。

2016年3月4日，有米科技在新三板完成一笔总金额为2.5亿元的融资，让陈第对新三板有了全新认识。他说，整个融资过程让人感受到了新三板的魅力。融资更是超出预期，实际谈融资时整个意向资金量达4亿多元，如果当时（发布《股票发行方案》时）不把融资额度限制在2.5亿元或以下，融资额可能会更高；融资效率也非常高，融资2.5亿元仅用一个半月，不用跟VC一家一家谈，效率提高很多。

对于未来的战略，陈第描绘了“一横多纵”的蓝图：有米以全球化的移动广告平台作为“横”线，将业务做广；借助移动广告平台的优势，重点布局游戏、电商、金融、教育、O2O等行业作为“纵”线，将业务做深，形成产业上下游的聚集，形成有米独有的生态流量网络。而对于移动广告这条“横”线本身，陈第对于有米发展战略的初衷表现出坚定而强烈的信心：“我们服务的广告主，最初很多都是APP广告主，现在我们做了延伸，这些广告主包含传统的品牌，可能会推广网页、微信或者市场活动。此外开发者也做了相应的延伸，以前是中小APP，现在是大的APP，还有微信公众号，包括自媒体号等等。”

王锐旭：向总理提建议的90后CEO

2015年1月27日上午，中南海的一间会议室，国务院总理李克强主持召开科教文卫人士和基层群众代表的座谈会。王锐旭带着发言稿、笔记本和笔，在工作人员的带领下，到了中南海里其中一间会议室。“每个人的座位早已安排好，而且座位前放着发言名单、发言顺序等。”

王锐旭说，除了看到自己排在第七位发言之外，他才注意到自己是广东地区的唯一代表，也是参会代表中最年轻的一个，与他一起出席会议的，还有姚明、陈道明、许宁生等，一共10人。

“直到那一刻，我才完全了解会议的内容：李克强总理主持召开座谈会，听取教育、科技、文化、卫生、体育界人士和基层群众代表对《政府工作报告（征求意见稿）》的意见和建议。”王锐旭说。

“坐下不久后，总理就走进会议室，微笑着跟每个参会代表握手。”王锐旭说，与总理见面握手的场景，虽然在心中早已排练过无数次，但当真正与总理握手介绍自己的时候，还是觉得非常紧张，手心也一直冒汗，“但依然能感受到总理的亲和力”。

“轮到我发言的时候，紧张的心情已经平静下来了。”王锐旭虽然准备了发言稿，但他发言的时候基本上是脱稿发言，“主要内容就是结合自身经历对大学生创业提了建议，希望落实大学生创业扶持政策，为大学生创业者创造实现梦想的条件。”

“总理现场回应说，促进大众创业、万众创新，大学生是其中的重要力量，要为他们实现梦想和自身价值‘铺路搭桥’、创造条件。”王锐旭说。

而在2月6日傍晚，王锐旭也在朋友圈转发了一条题为《陈道明为何被总理邀请进中南海座谈》的消息，并且留言称“能和陈老师坐一席真幸福”。

“在1月27日晚上的《新闻联播》播出大概5分钟后，我们客服就收到一家媒体的电话，想要对我们进行采访。在接下来的20分钟里面，我们陆陆续续接到近十家媒体的约访电话。”在王锐旭创办的公司中担任媒体推广工作的Ellen说，“几乎所有媒体都向我们提了这样一个问题：王锐旭是凭借什么作为90后创业代表去北京参加座谈会的？”

对此，兼职猫的创业团队给出了“霸气”的回应：没有抢占朋友圈，也没有高调秀融资，更没有其他花边新闻，比起狂妄、嚣张、幼稚等这些给90后的标签，相信大家更希望看到90后奋勇、坚韧、踏实、拼搏的一面，而王锐旭只是刚好做了一个表率，坚持做最努力最拼搏的90后创业青年。

参加总理的座谈会后，王锐旭人气爆棚，但他工作上基本没什么变化，似乎这几天的事从未发生过。1月29日上午，他照常上班；下午，他出现在共青团与人大代表、政协委员面对面暨市政协十二届四次会议提案交流会现场。王锐旭就建设一站式服务孵化基地建议：“希望孵化基地能够建设得更具公益性，少一些商业元素，并且提供包括大学生政策申办服务在内的一站式扶持服务。”

王锐旭刚刚从广州中医药大学毕业才半年，他大三时创立的广州九尾信息科技有限公司已顺利拿下了第二轮天使投资和千万级的A轮融资，公司估值过亿元。但少有人想到，如今的年轻CEO是曾经的网瘾少年，逆袭后在大学期间学业与事业共赢。从网瘾少年、大学生创业者到总理的座上宾，他的历程就是一本“励志小说”。

确实，王锐旭有着不一般的“履历”：除了在广州中医药大学期间5次获得奖学金，还曾经荣获“中国优秀科普志愿者”“千名志愿者”称号，获得首届广州青年创意创业大赛一等奖、2014“挑战杯”广东省创业实践赛金奖、“粤港澳”移动互联网设计大赛一等奖、校药膳大赛一等奖等30多个奖项，并获创新创业训练项目国家、省级立项各一项……他是学业与事业两不误的创业青年典型。

他的创业经历更加非同一般，做的是手机应用APP，大学读的却是与此毫不搭边的“中药资源与开发专业”。他在创业前做过保安、摆地摊等兼职工作；大二成立魔灯团队为企业进行校园品牌推广；大三时用自己积攒的7万元创办九尾信息科技有限公司，组建了一个由15人组成的创业团队，主推“兼职猫”，供大学生在上面搜寻各种安全可靠的兼职信息。他曾用一份8角钱打印出来的兼职方案，赢得了创业的第一桶金。

让人万万想不到的是，王锐旭曾是“网瘾少年”。王锐旭出生在汕头，家里经营羊毛生意，开了厂房，他11岁就在工厂帮父母“管账”。上初中后，王锐旭成了网吧的常客，几乎每天都要待上几个小时，“有一次为了网游通关，五一假期七天和弟弟泡在网吧里，每人轮流打游戏12小时，甚至饭都顾不上吃。”王锐旭回忆，不久之后，自己成了不折不扣的问题少年，网游、吸烟、喝酒、逃课样样均沾。祸不单行，中考前，家中工厂突遇危机，欠下巨额债务，家里破产。初三毕业，王锐旭拿着280分的中考成绩单走到母亲面前时，母亲打了他一记响亮的耳光，“妈妈哭了，可以想象她有多伤心和无助。”王锐旭被拉回残酷的现实，他开始意识到要挑起家里的重担。

于是他提出要接手父亲的工厂，不料遭到父亲的强烈反对。“他自己没有文化，所以不想我们走他的老路。”王锐旭说。

王锐旭被送回初中复读。父母也一改以往放养式的教育方式，加强对他学习的监督，为了帮助他戒掉网瘾，特意把他送到附近没有网吧的中学复读。

王锐旭戒掉了网瘾，埋头苦读，第二年考上了汕头华侨中学，高考考上了广州中医药大学。

大一时，王锐旭遇到心仪的女孩，因为谈恋爱，生活费明显不够用，当打电话回家要生活费时，他听出电话那头母亲的失望，家里因破产依旧债台高筑，“我骨子里有潮汕的大男子主义，潜意识里会想到要保护好母亲，不能让母亲为我而伤心”。王锐旭痛下决心，要自己赚钱。一心找兼职的他却先后遭遇了“交培训费”“办100元的工卡”“交兼职服装费”等五花八门的骗术，被黑中介骗走不少中介费。

在广州中医药大学，王旭锐开始创业。他的办公桌长1.5米，宽0.6米，在食堂靠东面，能坐下4个人。在这张桌子上，王锐旭“收复”了一个一个团队成员，他们组建了魔灯团队，和小伙伴们努力创业。“那时候，食堂阿姨对我笑笑，也是种莫大的鼓励。”

委屈、白眼、苦头、坚持、拼搏，换来了业务的上升，团队人数也从“二人传”升级为“四十人合唱团”，月收入也从零升到15万元。也是在这张桌子上，王锐旭开始了对未来的思考。在团队发展的压力下，出于对大学生兼职市场的耿耿于怀，王锐旭成立了九尾信息科技有限公司，并启动了大学生兼职平台——兼职猫的开发。那时的资金并不足以支撑技术研发，于是除了技术团队，所有人又投入了新一轮的校园代理和兼职工作中，只是为了一个简单得不能再简单的目的：养活技术团队。

2013年，他拥有了第二张桌子长2米，宽0.8米，有一部电话，有一台电脑，还有一群志同道合的创业青年。

它的位置坐落于白云区一个创意产业园，是团市委专门为广州青年就业创业发展提供的免费服务场地。

首届广州青年创意创业大赛，团市委邀请了一批专家和风投来“相马”。作为一匹受人瞩目的“黑马”，王锐旭被相中了，不仅获得创业大赛冠军，还获得一笔风投融资。

正是这些找兼职被骗的“惨痛经历”，催生了王锐旭做“兼职猫”的念头。也正因此，他创办的“兼职猫”非常重视发布信息的真实性。而今，在王锐旭的带领下，“兼职猫”的用户已有百万，并在前段时间顺利拿下了第二轮天使投资和千万级的A轮融资。面对互联网激烈的“同质竞争”问题时，王锐旭自信地说：“这样反而会更加激发大家的潜能，把这一领域做得更好。”

他表示，创业是为了赚钱，作为公司CEO的他有责任让创业团队过上好生活。“所以，不赚钱的创业都是耍流氓的”。

“作为从农村走出来的草根90后，我很珍惜。”王锐旭用行动给90后贴上了新标签：奋勇、坚韧、踏实、拼搏。创业前期，作为团队CEO的王锐旭需要全盘负责推广、运营、公关等事务，“我的工作很杂，哪里需要帮忙就过去帮忙，作为领导者要带领大家”。而今，公司部门职能区分越来越清晰，团队也不断壮大，王锐旭主要负责统筹公司的工作。

王锐旭非常勤奋刻苦，基本每天从上午9点开始工作到晚上12点，“好像一个人能做十个人的事，还经常帮忙做其他工作。”王锐旭在北京时因水土不服身体出现不适现象，但是第二天他依旧坚持上班、出席被邀请的会议。对此，他的解释是：“我现在是创业者，就必须学会承担这一身份带来的所有责任。至于工作方面，我有身边的伙伴陪伴着，和他们一起奋斗，这让我感觉很好”。

王锐旭表示，有关创业的活动，被邀请了，他一般都会参加。1月27日上午的座谈会给王锐旭带来了更多的目光，但是对他和他的团队来说，低调做人，高调做事才是始终不变的原则。他一再提醒同事：要继续努力，千万不要骄傲，要踏实地做好产品。

蒲少涛：尿毒症逼我去创业

2015年5月中旬，华南理工大学的基金会账号收到20万元。看到捐款人姓名——蒲少涛，负责的老师有些吃惊。这位2005级的校友大二时被检查出尿毒症，在学校和同学的帮助下，凭借自强不息的毅力完成学业。他的病情维持治疗花销不菲，20万元从何而来?

2005年，蒲少涛从陕西农村考入华南理工大学，成为一名光荣的国防生，踌躇满志之时，却在2006年年底查出患有尿毒症。蒲少涛没有怨天尤人，而是坚强面对病情。当时，无论是选择换肾还是透析治疗，数十万元的医疗费对于蒲少涛和远在偏僻乡村的家庭而言，都是无法承受的。蒲少涛一直靠勤工助学自己挣生活费，为了省车费他甚至很少回家。在医院接受治疗期间，蒲少涛乐观自信，为配合治疗，他坚持一天只喝一口水，前前后后十余次血液透析治疗，每次都痛得全身直发抖，他从没喊过一声苦。学校的老师同学得知消息后，在他入院的第二天就筹到3万多元捐款，随后又多次组织募捐、义演、义卖活动：有的同学在饭堂义卖自己的美术作品，有的同学捐出自己整整半年的家教收入，有的同学自发组织策划爱心义演，有的同学为他建立了一个网站，专门通告他的病情并呼吁救助……学校也成立了爱心基金，对他进行帮助。

经过一年多的治疗，他的病基本好转。出院后的蒲少涛重返学校，学校为蒲少涛提供了一间单人宿舍，他坚持每天四次、每次半小时的治疗，每天起床后第一件事就是为自己进行透析治疗，然后去上课，中午回到宿舍又接着做透析，下午下课后做第三次，晚上睡前还得再做一次。给伤口换药、给房子消毒，按时打针吃药也是他一手搞定。

未来看似黯淡，但蒲少涛并未自暴自弃，总是尽力做好力所能及的事。由于身体原因，蒲少涛不得不放弃国防生资格，课余时间多了起来，他便自学钟爱的计算机编程。“我得学个一技之长。”蒲少涛开始为自己考虑，于是选修了计算机专业的课程，还上网找教程学习。

如果那时有人经过蒲少涛的宿舍，经常可以看到他一边做治疗，一边手敲键盘。“学编程的时候，感觉治疗的时间过得飞快。”蒲少涛笑着说，学习也转移了对治疗压力的注意力。

有一次，听到老师说想找人将国防生网站改版，蒲少涛心头一热，便毛遂自荐。现在他做一个网站一个星期便能搞定，但当时由于技术不熟练，花了一个月的时间才把网站做出来。“硬着头皮把作品交上去”，老师却觉得新网站效果挺好。知道了蒲少涛网页设计的技能，老师们热情地介绍新的“客户”给他，在校期间，蒲少涛给学校十几个学院设计了网站，还接到些外校的单子。“兼职”帮蒲少涛赚取了一定的生活费，更重要的，是让他增添了生活的自信心。

在2007年度“中国大学生自强之星”评选中，蒲少涛高票当选。

虽然获取不小的荣誉，但强烈的生存危机还是摆在面前。蒲少涛对未来的期许是，找一份工作养活自己。他从未想过创业，直到面临“毕业即失业”的尴尬。

2009年在金融危机扫荡下，应届毕业生面临前所未有的艰难就业季。尽管如此，凭借扎实的编程技术，有好几个不错的软件开发类岗位向蒲少涛抛出橄榄枝。是否要隐瞒病情？蒲少涛在心里挣扎过，最终还是选择诚实告知。

一个公司打电话让他去报到，他将病情告知对方，并再三保证：身体不影响工作，以后病情与公司无任何关系。但对方还是回绝了他。“我理解企业的做法。”蒲少涛叹了一口气说，“但看到其他同学都在讨论找到的工作，心里还是挺失落的。”至此，蒲少涛断了找工作的念头。

别人创业大多是出于兴趣，或追逐理想，但对蒲少涛而言，创业是被迫无奈的选择。恰在这时，学校老师给蒲少涛送来一个好消息：省里正支持大学生自主创业，对于符合条件的学生可以提供一笔启动资金。为此，蒲少涛拿到了10万元的创业启动资金。

毕业后，在与别人合租的民宅里，“光杆司令”蒲少涛开始了网站设计与维护的创业项目。由于缺少资金，他一直在犹豫是否招人，“人来了没项目怎么办呢”。但不迈出第一步，永远不能获得成功。最终，蒲少涛破釜沉舟般招了4名员工，搬进另一个140平方米的民宅。压力大，很多事情必须亲力亲为，蒲少涛的身体备受考验。有一天晚上10点钟，他给客户送展板，回来时已经没公交车了。那天天空下着大雨，他走了半个小时，腿都抽筋了。“经常为了几百元的订单熬夜”，蒲少涛很拼，因为他没有退路。

一年多下来，去掉员工工资和各项投入，蒲少涛发现自己并没有赚到钱。2011年，听从哥哥的建议，蒲少涛把目光投向了电商，成为天猫最早做建材与家居产品网上定制与销售的商家。由于发展需要，他将创业战场从广州搬迁到了清远，注册成立了清新乐友家居用品有限公司，存储仓库从最初的一两百平方米，扩大到1000多平方米，发展至今已成为一家专业的窗轨供应商。

随着同类型网店越来越多，价格战导致利润降低，不利于公司长久发展。蒲少涛从营销模式和服务质量突围，希望成就“独一无二”。公司在全国布局了线下服务网络，“从广州找一个师傅开始，半年时间新疆、西藏都有了人，只要订单一下，师傅就上门进行窗帘的专业安装服务”。

蒲少涛还开发了一套ERP系统，专门用于定制类订单管理。早期用普通的网店销售系统，客户每改一个意见，就需要人工对照表格进行定价改动，效率低且容易出错。改进系统后，大大减轻工作量，“之前得15个销售人员才能完成的工作，目前只需要10个人”。

为了更好地为顾客服务，公司还提出了“20元规则”：即顾客收货发现产品有不满意之处（如颜色有差别），公司会给予买家几元到20元的赔偿。因此，有的买家只是买了10元的产品，都有可能获得20元的赔偿。

优质的产品与客户体验，蒲少涛的“致尚家居”旗舰店成为天猫窗帘配件销售第一品牌。从2012年开始，“致尚家居”已是天猫KA级商家。产品可以复制，服务可以模仿，公司要长久发展，转型升级、掌握核心技术是关键。蒲少涛把目光转向智能家居，尝试通过手机控制整个家居的带电产品，目前硬件设备正在测试。蒲少涛说：“如果可行，顾客回家前就可以通过手机APP先开好空调、放好洗澡水。”蒲少涛形容，“这就像给现在的产品装上大脑。”

公司走上正轨后，蒲少涛以更加实在的方式回报社会。在粤北的清远市，蒲少涛公司的员工大多数学历不高，许多都是高中毕业生，但平均月收入能拿到四五千元，有些勤奋的甚至能拿到上万元，“买房都不是难事”。每年公司会给员工安排体检，也设立奖金奖励优秀员工。另外，网店每一笔订单成交额的千分之一，将会捐助给贫困山区小孩供其上学；蒲少涛还想为陕西农村的农产品打通网上销售渠道，希望农民可以多挣一点钱。

终于攒到一些家产了，蒲少涛不声不响地给华南理工大学基金会账号汇款20万元，希望用于重病学生的帮扶。蒲少涛说：“在我最困难的时候，学校和社会给了我巨大的关爱和帮助，现在我有了一定的能力，要将这份关爱和帮助传递下去。”

工厂、村庄
遭遇互联网

厂区新生途径：互联网+！文化+！

随着厂里广播的响起，工人们下班了。有师傅骑着自行车，载着老婆，去厂里的菜市场买菜。有师傅端着陶瓷茶盅，穿着厂服，戴着白手套，准备去厂里的小学接孩子放学。这是属于20世纪80年代广州工业大道老工厂的记忆。

互联网+纺织机械厂里的微信总部

今天名震华南、微信总部所在的TIT创意园，前身是1956年成立的广州纺织机械厂，也是当时华南地区最大的纺织机械厂。

今天，改造后的TIT创意园既有着老厂房的沧桑感，又带着现代建筑的冷峻时尚。从艺苑路的正门进入园区，10面长方形板墙按照冷色调到暖色调一字排开，方板中间镂空出世界各地不同特色的服装模特造型。园区之内，21座古朴的工业厂房、纵横交错的管道线网和和造型独特的雕塑及工业机械模型，穿插在300多株参天大树之间，交织成别具一格的办公空间。绯色斑斓的工厂砖墙上，印着带有浓郁时代特色的壁画及标语“工农群众知识化，知识分子劳动化”，种种旧工业印记让人像是回到了30年前。

园区的服装相关企业有十多家，其余的企业则包括了网络科技、影视传媒、建筑设计、餐饮酒吧等。其中，最知名的腾讯微信总部两年前进驻，如今占据了超过五座厂房。

三三两两的员工在公司旁露天咖啡馆开会，程序员们在电脑前疯狂敲打着键盘……这样的情景在TIT并不鲜见。相比之下，服装商铺的生意显得有些冷清。园区内的服装企业大多走中高端路线，定位为“顶级”“定制”的高级服装会所，服装价格在800～2000元。

厂区转身，迈向电商产业园，城市的历史记忆在这里驻足，波澜壮阔的二次创业史由此拉开。

地处广州新中轴线南段的海珠区，在沿线形成了“广州南中轴电子商务大道”，成为“互联网+”主战场。其中，广一国际电子商务产业园正是从原广州第一水泵厂厂房改造而来。该园区占地面积3.8万平方米，重点入驻优秀大型企业总部、孵化优秀种子企业，享受海珠区电子商务有关扶持优惠政策，定位为建成文化与科技相融合的国家级电子商务示范园区，目前园区入驻企业45家，在孵企业19家。

这样的改造模式，既保留了“广一”字号和风貌，更成为海珠区“退二进三”标志性工程。

快速发展中的广一电商园区雄心勃勃：计划通过三年时间，改造修建创意办公建筑3万～5万平方米，引入3～5家知名的电子商务示范企业，集聚100家中小电子商务企业。在园区实现年产值密度10万元/平方米、纳税密度5000元/平方米以上，入驻企业年总产值超10亿元，纳税1.5亿元以上。运营方“五行集群”是电商、科技、创意园区开发、运营专业机构。有关负责人张民旭说，在厂区升级为电商园区的过程中，物理空间只是基础，为总部企业、种子企业供应政务支持、创投、行业协作、创业氛围这些服务“催化剂”，创造企业易于成功的“化学空间”更为重要。

“比如一个企业，为什么不在天河北、珠江新城的写字楼办公，要到园区办公？租金是一个因素，员工的工作状态、创意空间、创新社群，是更重要的部分。”

张民旭认为，老工厂转型新电商园，必须深深植根所在地经济升级和城市升级两大土壤，真正实现从“物理空间”到“化学空间”的转变。

文化+博物馆引领，人民印刷厂正在设计最前沿产品

在“退二进三”战略席卷广州的同时，创意产业开始崛起。老工厂区开始升华了。

作为“一个以国际标准定义的艺术、生活中心”，红专厂依然保存浓烈的工厂气氛。现在，这里有国内外知名的画廊、设计工作室、艺术展示空间、时尚店铺、特色餐厅及咖啡厅，这里还有“休闲文艺的小清新”。文艺青年们充满感情地写道：“一个人的时候，你会爱上这里。”

1956年，中国最大的罐头厂“广东罐头厂”诞生于此。1994年，更名为“广州鹰金钱企业集团公司”，在“退二进三”中，鹰金钱搬迁，艺术家们将废弃的生产车间改造成了LOFT风格街区。

木板印刷的古画、铜活字印刷的模型、儿时常见的油墨印刷设备、用盐水就能发光的手电筒……位于燕子岗南路的广州市人民印刷厂也是工业大道沿线的工业记忆之一。当印刷生产搬离海珠之后，这个老厂的招牌并未离去，静静变身成“包装印刷文化创意产

业园”，包括讲述印刷历史的广州印刷博物馆，防伪技术研发中心和工业包装设计研发基地。

有60年历史的广州市人民印刷厂，对于不少广州人来说都十分熟悉。当年的粮票、油票、债券、税票、户口簿就是在这里印刷的。早些年开始，人民印刷厂已经悄然转型，主要的印刷生产搬到了白云区，而位于海珠区的老厂区，变身成为广东省第一个印刷文化创意产业园。

走进印刷文化创意产业园，最吸引人的是这里的广州印刷博览馆。八百平方米的展览馆，原来是一个堆放印刷油墨和纸张的仓库，现在则浓缩地展示了从甲骨文到最先进的数码印刷的整个印刷历史。在现场，不仅可以看到众多木板印刷、活字印刷的实物，还有人现场演示唐朝最风行的雕版佛经印刷。

在现场还看到不少年代久远的印刷机器，据人民印刷厂负责人介绍，这些都是过去人民印刷厂留下来的老机器。其中还有许多老一辈人都熟悉的油墨印刷设备——在一张蜡纸上刻字，然后用蘸了油墨的刷子一刷，墨就印到纸上变成文字。20世纪七八十年代上学的人，小时候都做过这种油墨印刷的试卷。目前博物馆申报爱国主义和科普教育基地。

而在博物馆的二楼，则是现代最新的工业包装设计理念的代表。展馆中的一件展品很有趣，加进约300毫升的淡盐水，这个手电筒就可以发光100个小时，“加海水甚至尿液都能使用，是应急的首选”设计者一边演示一边介绍这种具有专利的盐水灯，一经推出就接到了日本的大量订单，成为日本地震应急包中的必备品。

与工业包装设计中心相邻的是产业园的核心——防伪技术研发中心，目前已经研发出数十种防伪技术应用在包装设计上。世界知名的惠普（HP）公司也在创意园内开设印刷品展示中心。

印刷博物馆所在的创意产业园分三期进行改造，总占地面积1.08万平方米，总投资达到1.5亿元。除了印刷博览馆，还形成高新技术研发区、文化创意设计区、专利技术孵化区、防伪技术应用中心，聚集一批与印刷相关的高新科技研发企业和文化创意企业、包装设计企业。

旧记忆“工厂博物馆”记录广州创业史

当电商园、创意园崛起，广州辉煌的工业发展史却并未被遗忘。

今年75岁的老工人黄师傅，常常会到创意园散步。他1968年进入广州纺织机械厂工作，刚进入工厂时，厂房附近都是竹林，十分荒凉，“90年代中期是最辉煌的时候，全厂1300多名员工，一个厂长、九个副厂长，很多工人戏称他们为‘十大元帅’。”

半个世纪的光景，这里的英雄已经从“工厂元帅”变成了创意达人。黄师傅十分欣慰：“老厂倒闭关门之后，没想到大部分厂房都被保留了下来。还记得我以前在供应科的厂房，现在变成了一家酒店。”

正在附近补习学校备考雅思的大学生小尚带着北京的朋友专程来参观TIT，小尚的介绍简单有力，“这就是广州的798。”在创意园北面，TIT二期正如火如荼地建设着。

在工业大道中313号，大门处硕大的“东方红”三个字似乎将人牵引回往日时光。东方红印刷厂组建于1968年，20世纪90年代起，新印刷企业遍地开花，那时候东方红有“印刷的黄埔军校”一说，吸引了很多人来做学徒。后来公司不景气，有私企印刷厂跑来挖技术人员，只要穿着东方红的工作服去面试，不用考试就可以通过。

2009年，东方红关闭了印铁车间，搬出广州。现在拱门上的“东方红”鲜艳醒目依旧，不过已经成为“东方红创意园”的招牌。旧厂房被完整保留，砖墙上还残留着种种标语，园区里已经到处是摄影会所、网络公司，还有让人有些摸不着头脑的“品牌疑难研究所”……老厂房变了，园区里不再是统一制服的工人，而是慕名而来的游客，奇装异服的时装模特。

曾经辉煌的广州工业发展史打动着每一个造访者。位于白鹅潭西岸、毓灵古桥旁的协同和机器厂在中国历史上赫赫有名。1915年，这里制造出中国第一台柴油机，扛起了中国近代民族工业的一面大旗。新中国成立后，这里成为广州柴油机厂的一部分。2011年，这个百年老厂房退出了工业生产，变身为“柴油机博物馆”，以老机器为背景展出当年工人们挥汗奋斗的历史场景。

随着工业发展和更新换代，旧生产工具和资料被不断淘汰。有心将其保存下来的，反而成就了今天的“工厂博物馆”。

“淘宝”潮涌广东农村

夜里将近12点，广东揭阳市的军埔村显得十分安静。在村里著名的智慧大街上，多数网络批发店早已关门，偶尔透过门缝能看到一些店里包装好的服装码得整整齐齐，堆积如山。作为省内最出名的淘宝村之一，2016年的“双十一”网购狂欢节，军埔村电商销售额超过了8000万元。军埔村电商的崛起，是广东东区打造大军埔电商圈的一环。从这里流传开去的发展经验，正被广泛复制到揭阳的城市和农村。

军埔村位于揭东区锡场镇，面积仅0.53平方公里，现有家庭490户，2800多人。全村目前已有350多户近2000人投入网上销售活动，开设各类网店3000多家、实体网批店320多家。在这里，基本上除了小孩和年纪太大的老人家，所有村民都在做电商，很多家庭主妇上了政府开设的免费电商培训班之后，也开起了网店。现在已经很少有人知道军埔曾是个社会矛盾突出的“问题村”。转变源于三年前，几名在广州打工的本村年轻人返乡开淘宝店创业。随后引来无数村民效仿，军埔村的人气越来越旺，名气越来越大，成为电商巨头阿里巴巴认证的“淘宝村”之一。

目前，大军埔电商圈已具雏形。军埔电商模式作为一种可复制的经验，已被揭阳市政府推广到全市农村。

对，农村，这两个字前所未有地和互联网挨得这么近！2017年2月15日，中国商务部就全国农产品市场体系建设情况发布信息：2016年我国农产品电商交易额预计突破2200亿元。对广东“村里人”来说，这是一块肥沃的新土地。在热气腾腾的“农产品电商”网络末端，越来越多的乡村小店成为电商企业的村级服务站，承担着快递包裹收寄、中转的重要作用。

“一天至少有十来单货。”广东韶关始兴县太平镇一家加入该网络的村级服务站小店店主邹婷婷在记者面前兴高采烈。她说，现在的网购单子主要为家电、服装和一些日用品，平时靠电动三轮车就可以送货了，物流压力并不大，而自己每月也有两三千块钱的提成。

2016年，广东提出到2020年，全省农村电子商务应用水平显著提高，农村电子商务支撑服务体系基本建立，城乡产品双向流通渠道基本形成，农产品网络销售及农村网络购物规模持续扩大，整体发展水平居全国前列。在全省建成50个县级电子商务产业园和100个乡镇电子商务运营中心，实现农村电子商务服务站在行政村全覆盖。以电子商务、信息化及物流网络为依托，以“万村千乡市场工程”为基础，加快推进农村现代流通网络建设，加强商贸流通、供销、邮政等系统物流服务网络和设施建设与衔接，畅通日用消费品下乡进村渠道。

从农村考到城市的大学生们，也在竭尽所能，让父老乡亲享受互联网红利。暨大的农村学生袁森林，大二暑假在梅州兴宁调研时听到一个小故事：一位在东莞上班的儿子特意为家乡的老父亲寄来了公司分发的粽子。但是乡镇间物流的不畅通，父亲又很少接收邮件，这次快递直接变成了“慢递”。满怀儿子心意的粽子送达父亲手中时，已经变质不能食用。

袁森林和另外四名同在农村成长、在城市学习的“90后”于是组队立项，建设“乡镇通”平台。五个年轻人思想很一致：现阶段农村物流和电商发展比较落后，农村的农产品难以运送到城市，城市的实用商品也难以运送到农村。他的团队希望打造一个为农民提供电商服务来联结农村人口和城镇人口的物质纽带。结合调研和所学知识，他们将“乡镇通”的服务分为乡镇物流代理和网络平台代购两个方面：在物流方面，将在县城设置县区总仓，统一代收快件，并与便利店合作，实现客户自行到代理点取件；在代购方面，开发了农民导购平台，让农民能够“网购”。

这个小团队开始为新年的“挑战杯”全国大学生创业大赛做准备。从立项到参赛的两年时间里，“乡镇通”团队为调研走遍了广东省内如罗岗、叶塘等的20多个乡镇。在汕尾市的一个农村，学生们遇到了一位老人。老人的儿女外出打工，常年不在家，家中地里种植了龙眼树。龙眼收购价格很低，再加上老人年事已高，家中大片的龙眼无人采摘，常常在树上烂掉。袁森林的团队征得了老人的同意后采摘了100斤的龙眼带回深圳上网销售，短短50分钟的时间，100斤新鲜的龙眼被抢购一空。

“‘龙眼’销售体现的正是中国农村中普遍存在的一个问题：高质的农产品难以送达城市，造成的不只是农民的收入问题，还会导致资源的浪费。‘乡镇通’的构想解决的就是‘输出’和‘送达’的问题。”于是，作为中转中心的快递行业又成了“乡镇通”团队调研的重点……

看好广东农村电商事业的当然还有很多人。“农村电商是有前途的屌丝。”广东亚太电子商务研究院院长陈海权在媒体面前如是评价。他说，广东农村电商交易额保守估计2017年能达到280亿元，2020年将达到430亿元。广东有很多特色农产品，全省85%左右的县已经形成花卉、蔬果、水产、肉类特色涉农产业。而且广东不仅仅是农产品产量大，更是省外农产品重要的消费地和集散地。

城中村的互联网梦想

2016年9月23日，中国青年创业就业基金会与广州市天河区政府签订战略合作框架协议书，将在天河区的21个街道都建设5000~30000平方米规模不等的中国青年创业社区。这也意味着全省首个中国青年创业社区“5ipark”将落户广州市天河区。

5ipark互联网青年创业社区是由五行孵化器集团、IDG资本、中国青年创业就业基金会联合发起的互联网孵化器品牌，她坚定选择在广东落户，有着充足的理由。

共青团中央中国青年创业就业基金会秘书长陈宗雄心勃勃：“这是中国青年创业社区在全国首个与区级行政单位的合作项目，希望能在天河区做区一级行政单元合作的全国示范，未来可复制推广”。他说，中国青年创业社区集创业赛事、创业培训、创业服务、创业金融、创业社交、创业推广和创业征信于一体，为创业青年建造创业办公、居住生活、休闲娱乐的创业“微城”，这一次首次落户广东省，选择天河区为第一个站点，是因为天河区在IT产业、互联网产业方面在全国具备领先优势。与此同时，天河区一直在推动城中村孵化器建设，未来将拿出约400万平方米的城中村物业改造为众创空间。

根据协议，双方共同推进实施“中国青年创业社区及子品牌5ipark互联网青年创业社区”项目，在天河区推动及创建“一街道一社区”的示范发展模式，即在天河区21个街道中，力争在每个街道建设5000～30000平方米规模不等的青创社区，形成青年双创孵化服务体系及青年创新创业人才库，提供资源集中孵化，令各街道创业企业各具特色又互补，形成规模效应。

此外，每个青创社区都将划出一定面积建设众创空间，为创客群体提供全免费的工位及基础孵化培育服务，力争2年内在天河区实现3000个免费工位。双方还将建立中国青年创业就业基金天河子基金，专项用于投资支持入驻青创社区双创项目及团队。

“5ipark青创社区在天河区建设的范本，将建成集5i创新工场、5i孵化器、5i加速器、5i创业公寓和5i创意街于一体的复合孵化器。”5ipark互联网青年创业社区联合创始人张民旭说，5ipark打造多种维度的社区文化体系，从多元化的社区组合、多样性的城市新空间、地区及行业影响力强大的活动、专门的社员入社评审和服务、跨区域跨行业跨界的资源嫁接。“这不仅要构造一个耳目一新的社区空间，更重要的是要与入驻企业和人群一起，构造城市中更先进的工作和生活形态。”张民旭解释，“5ipark社区是盛行一时的众创空间、创客空间的迭代产品，是创新型孵化器。”

在南粤都市，城中村们激发着越来越强烈的新创业梦想。在广州中山大道西有一个棠下街，这是一个典型的城中村街道。7.42平方公里分布了棠下、棠东两个城中村，35万人居住在此，其中外来打工人员就有26万人，数量之多可居天河区城中村首位，日产垃圾

230吨，占天河区垃圾总量的1/6。和广州的大部分城中村近似，棠下街道路狭隘，崎岖不平，转角处随处可见乱丢弃的垃圾，各类电线纵横密布。

要让这里也能生长出孵化器，街道先后拆除南边大街、大片路、东南路、三担街、毓桂大街、官育路、口岗大街、丰乐路、富华街等街巷的占道梯级和铁架，拓宽和新铺沥青路面近3500多米，修建人行道3000米，安装交通栏4200米，疏通和新铺150条街巷下水道，解决26处长期困扰群众出行的水浸街黑点；“微循环”管理模式也随之引进，4条封闭式管理的车行道路使车辆能在村内按交通标志有序循环运行，500多个高清摄像头优化设置……有序的建设带动当地物业的租金水平提高了30%，同时也吸引了一批市场前景好、创新能力强的高科技企业进驻。棠下街用3个月的时间，重点对村公司现有物业周边的环境进行集中整治，之后在棠下街辖棠东东路棠东村旧厂房园区，形成了一定规模的新三板孵化基地。

“村里的众创空间”建设现在还在天河持续推进。在全区约1100万平方米的村集体物业中，拿出约1/3改造为平价高效、设计新颖的创新发展空间。城中村的创新聚变效应正在显现。天河区用较低的创业成本、较完善的创业创新服务链条，对数以万计的创新创业者敞开怀抱。同时，天河区城中村的村民从原先出租物业谋生到加入新经济大潮，一些村集体经济组织甚至参与到互联网生态家园项目的投资中，成为全球创新链的一环。

图书在版编目（CIP）数据

创新的广东 / 陈翔著. —广州：广东人民出版社，2017.6
（中国梦·广东故事）
ISBN 978-7-218-11891-8

Ⅰ.①创… Ⅱ.①陈… Ⅲ.①企业创新—企业发展—广东 Ⅳ.①F279.276.5

中国版本图书馆CIP数据核字（2017）第128879号

CHUANGXIN DE GUANGDONG
创新的广东 陈翔 著

出 版 人：肖风华

总 撰 稿：刘 旦
责任编辑：黎 捷 王 宁
封面设计：李桢涛
责任技编：周 杰 吴彦斌

出版发行：广东人民出版社
地　　址：广州市大沙头四马路10号（邮政编码：510102）
电　　话：（020）83798714（总编室）
传　　真：（020）83780199
网　　址：http://www. gdpph. com
印　　刷：广东信源彩色印务有限公司
开　　本：787mm×1092mm 1/32
印　　张：6.5 字 数：200千
版　　次：2017年6月第1版 2017年6月第1次印刷
定　　价：60.00元

如发现印装质量问题，影响阅读，请与出版社(020-83795749)联系调换。
售书热线：（020）83795240